1000 Game of Thrones Facts

Scott Ambrose

© Copyright 2024 Scott Ambrose
All Rights Reserved

Contents

4 - Introduction
5 - 1000 Game of Thrones Facts

INTRODUCTION

Game of Thrones was a popular fantasy television series based on the A Song of Ice and Fire novels by George RR Martin.

The show premiered on HBO in 2011 and ran for eight seasons. It follows the power struggles between noble families as they fight for control of the Iron Throne in the fictional land of Westeros. The show was known for its complex characters, intricate plots, and shocking twists.

Delve deep into the intricate world of Westeros with this comprehensive fact book about the hit series. From the noble houses and their sigils to the blood-soaked battles and historical allusions, this book covers everything fans need to know about the epic fantasy saga. Actors, characters, behind the scenes, episodes, influences, differences from the books and so on.

All this and much more awaits in 1000 Game of Thrones facts.

1000 GAME OF THRONES FACTS

(1) One of the other child actors vying with Bella Ramsey for the Lyanna Mormont role in Game of Thrones was Millie Bobby Brown. It didn't turn out too bad for Brown though because she was cast as Eleven in Stranger Things that same year.

(2) The Accursed Kings series by Maurice Druon was an influence on George RR Martin. The Accursed Kings is a historical fiction series set in medieval France during the reign of King Philip IV. The series follows the power struggles, betrayals, and political intrigue of the French royal court, as various factions vie for control of the throne.

(3) If you include the battle sequences, it is estimated that around 150,000 characters died in Game of Thrones.

(4) Faye Marsay appeared in the 2014 Doctor Who Christmas special. Her character in the episode mentions planning a Game of Thrones marathon. A year later Faye Marsay was actually in Game of Thrones. She played the Waif - the character who torments Arya in Braavos.

(5) Game of Thrones became a merchandising juggernaut. This was somewhat unusual for something which was aimed at mature audiences.

(6) Liam Cunningham said he thought of his character Davos Seaworth as sort of like Tom Hagen in The Godfather. Tom Hagen is the Consigliere (adviser) to the Corleone family. He is a trusted and loyal member of the family who handles important decisions and negotiations on behalf of Don Vito Corleone. Hagen is known for his intelligence, calmness, and

ability to mediate conflicts. These are three qualities you can apply to Davos.

(7) Game of Thrones was jokingly pitched to HBO as 'The Sopranos meets Middle-Earth'.

(8) Arya serving Walder Fre his sons in a pie is inspired by Shakespeare's Titus Andronicus.

(9) The title sequence in Game of Thrones was inspired by a mechanical astrolabe, a historical instrument used to track the position of celestial bodies.

(10) The shield Jon Snow uses to protect himself from Ramsay Bolton's arrows at the end of Battle of the Bastards bears the sigil of House Mormont. House Mormont didn't have many soldiers but one of them evidently played a heroic and crucial role.

(11) The highest rated episode of Game of Thrones on IMDB is a three way dead heat between The Rains of Castamere, Battle of the Bastards, and The Winds of Winter. These episodes all have a near perfect 9.9 out of 10.

(12) The costume department on Game of Thrones had an embroidery team consisting of more than 40 people who sewed by hand to create the intricate designs on the costumes.

(13) Jerome Flynn, who played Bronn, had a lot of success in the mid 1990s with Robson & Jerome - a singing duo with fellow actor Robson Green (Jerome and Robson Green were in a popular drama show together called Soldier Soldier). Bronn gets to sing a few times in Game of Thrones.

(14) Game of Thrones is set in a medieval sort of world but it is deliberately anachronistic in a Horrible Histories, BlackAdder sort of way. Characters like Tyrion and Bronn often feel very contemporary in their language.

(15) Lena Headey said the Iron Throne in the show was very uncomfortable to sit on.

(16) When he did his audition for the part of Sandor "The Hound" Clegane, Rory McCann was working as a lumberjack and of no fixed abode.

(17) King's Landing is the capital city of the Seven Kingdoms. It is located on the eastern coast of Westeros and serves as the seat of the Iron Throne, the ruling monarchy of the realm. King's Landing is a bustling and highly populated city, known for its political intrigue, power struggles, and lavish lifestyles of the noble families who reside there. Life for ordinary folk is a bit less lavish though to say the least.

(18) Stannis Baratheon was partly based on Tiberius. Tiberius was a Roman emperor who ruled from 14 AD to 37 AD. He was known for his reclusive and paranoid nature.

(19) Wildfire is a highly dangerous and volatile substance created by the alchemists of King's Landing. It is described as a green, viscous liquid that ignites easily and burns with a distinctive green flame. Wildfire is used as a weapon of mass destruction, capable of causing massive devastation and destruction. We see this substance play a key role in Blackwater and The Winds of Winter.

(20) Patrick Malahide said that in his portrayal of Balon Greyjoy he made the character reflect his surroundings. Balon is therefore bleak and flinty.

(21) The lowest rated episode of Game of Thrones on IMDB is The Iron Throne - which has a dismal 4 out 10.

(22) Elizabeth Olsen unsuccessfully auditioned for the part of Daenerys Targaryen. Olsen later played Wanda Maximoff in the Marvel film universe.

(23) Maisie Williams said that when she started on Game of Thrones as a child she was asked to eat her lunch with a bib on so she wouldn't get food on her costume!

(24) Cersei blowing up the Great Sept of Baelor has some parallels with Guy Fawkes - although Fawkes didn't get that far. Guy Fawkes was a member of a group of English Catholics who conspired to blow up the Houses of Parliament in London in 1605, in what is now known as the Gunpowder Plot. The plot was an attempt to assassinate King James I, who was a Protestant, and restore a Catholic monarch to the throne. November 5th, the date of the failed Gunpowder Plot, is now commemorated in Britain as Bonfire Night with fireworks displays and the burning of effigies of Guy Fawkes on bonfires. The character V wears a Guy Fawkes mask in Alan Moore's V For Vendetta.

(25) The battle scene in Battle of the Bastards took nearly a month to shoot.

(26) Game of Thrones clearly takes some influence from I, Claudius. I, Claudius is a historical novel written by Robert Graves, first published in 1934. It is a fictional autobiography of the Roman emperor Claudius, who ruled from 41 to 54 AD. The novel is written as if it were Claudius' own memoirs, recounting his life from childhood to his unexpected rise to power. The book provides a detailed insight into the political intrigue and scandals of ancient Rome. The book was turned

into a brilliant television series by the BBC in 1976. The political intrigue and quest for power in Rome is a lot like the political intrigue and backstabbing we see in Kings Landing in Game of Thrones.

(27) Game of Thrones was based on George RR Martin's book series A Song of Ice and Fire.

(28) Liam Cunningham, despite being Irish, played Davos Seaworth with an excellent Geordie accent. A 'Geordie' accent is associated with the English city of Newcastle.

(29) Dan Weiss and David Benioff were showrunners, producers, and sometimes writers and directors on Game of Thrones. They were responsible for creating the show and adapting the books.

(30) A lot of fake snow was used in Game of Thrones - especially for Winterfell scenes. The fake snow was mostly made of paper.

(31) Game of Thrones was based at Titanic Studios in Belfast and took advantage of the lovely scenery available in the surrounding areas.

(32) In 2017 it was reported that over 300 baby girls in England had been given the name Arya in tribute to Game of Thrones.

(33) One of the interesting traditions in Game of Thrones was that the penultimate episode would be the big crazy one (more akin to a finale) and then the last episode would be like the aftermath.

(34) The War of the Roses was a big influence on the books

and show. The War of the Roses was a series of civil wars fought in England between two rival branches of the House of Plantagenet - the House of Lancaster and the House of York. The conflict lasted from 1455 to 1485 and was fought over the throne of England. The war was named after the badges of the two rival factions - the red rose of Lancaster and the white rose of York. The two sides were initially led by King Henry VI of the House of Lancaster and Richard, Duke of York from the House of York.

(35) Prior to season eight, only one episode of Games of Thrones scored less than 8 on IMDB. All of the episodes in season eight scored under 8 - with three of them scoring under 6. This did tend to illustrate the general perception that season eight marked a plunge in quality.

(36) For the death scene of Lyanna Mormont in Game of Thrones, Bella Ramsey had to be hoisted 25 feet in the air by a robotic claw (which was obviously then turned into a giant by CGI).

(37) Joffrey talks about the fate of Rhaenyra Targaryen in a Game of Thrones scene. In hindsight, this is actually a spoiler for the prequel show House of the Dragon!

(38) Hannah Murray, who played Gilly, and Jacob Anderson, who played Grey Worm, used to be flatmates before they were in Game of Thrones.

(39) Nathalie Emmanuel, who played Missandei, said she had to work a second job in retail on her early days on Game of Thrones because she didn't get paid much and had a mortgage.

(40) Fairhead in County Antrim was the location for the cliffs

you see in The Queen's Justice.

(41) Julian Glover, who played Maester Pycelle, said he asked to leave before season six because he felt there was nothing for his character to do and he was tired of playing scenes where Pycelle meekly gets humiliated by Cersei. Glover was persuaded to stay for one more season and said he's glad he did because he loved his death scene.

(42) The kind hearted Maester of Castle Black, Aemon (Targaryen), was memorably played by Peter Vaughan. Peter Vaughan was often known for playing villains and menacing characters in the past. British people knew him best as Grouty - the powerful crime boss in the 70s prison sitcom Porridge.

(43) The Wall along the northern border of Westeros was inspired by Hadrian's Wall. Hadrian's Wall is a famous historical site located in northern England, built by the Roman Emperor Hadrian in the 2nd century AD. The wall was the northernmost boundary of the Roman Empire at the time. It was constructed to defend the Roman province of Britannia against raids from the 'barbarian' tribes to the north.

(44) An ice cream store in Cornwall named Game of Cones got a nice surprise in 2022 when Emilia Clarke popped in for some ice cream.

(45) Maisie Williams was thirteen when the show began and twenty-one when it ended.

(46) The part of Hodor was the first acting job for Kristian Nairn. Kristian Nairn, who is from Northern Ireland, was a trance DJ before he became an actor.

(47) The Long Night episode in season eight required 55

consecutive night shoots to get in the can.

(48) Three different actors played Gregor (The Mountain) Clegane. Conan Stevens left due to a scheduling conflict and was replaced by Ian Whyte. Whyte only played the Mountain for a few episodes before being redeployed as a Wilding giant. The third actor to play the Mountain was the Icelandic strongman Hafþór Júlíus Björnsson. Björnsson is the person most associated with this part.

(49) Paddy Considine declined an audition for Game of Thrones because he wasn't interested in doing a fantasy show. He would of course years later play Viserys I Targaryen in the prequel show House of the Dragon.

(50) Stephen Dillane, who played Stannis Baratheon, said he never watched any of Game of Thrones because the show was too 'brutal' and violent for his tastes.

(51) Gwendoline Christie said she spent three months training for the fight scene between Brienne and the Hound.

(52) Peter Dinklage said that one of the things he most enjoyed about Northern Ireland was the excellent beer - which was stronger than American beer!

(53) The role of Olenna Tyrell was expanded from the books to take advantage of the towering and charismatic performance supplied by the late great Dame Diana Rigg.

(54) Over 12,000 wigs were used by the cast and extras during Game of Thrones.

(55) The Mongol empire was an influence on the Dothraki. The Mongol Empire was a vast empire that existed in the 13th

and 14th centuries, stretching from Eastern Europe to East Asia. It was founded by Genghis Khan in 1206. The Mongol Empire was known for its military prowess and ruthless conquests.

(56) The Stark family accents are what you might describe as mismatched. Sean Bean, Richard Madden and Kit Harington do northern (English) accents while Sophie Turner, Isaac Hempstead Wright and Maisie Williams speak in southern (RP) accents. It seems as if the actors were just allowed to use which accent they liked. Sean Bean is obviously using his real life Yorkshire accent in the show.

(57) The cast on Game of Thrones said that when they got new scripts the first thing they did was check to see if their character managed to survive!

(58) Joe Dempsie, who played Gendry, said that people would often get him muddled up with his friend Daniel Portman - who played Podrick.

(59) Game of Thrones follows multiple noble families in their quest for control of the Iron Throne.

(60) Gwendoline Christie, who played Brienne of Tarth, is 6'3 in real life.

(61) Mark Addy said he enjoyed shooting King Robert Baratheon's death scenes because it was a cold studio but he was in a nice warm bed!

(62) Tamzin Merchant played Daenerys Targaryen in the unaired pilot. This part was obviously recast when the series went ahead.

(63) Tamzin Merchant has since said she was glad she didn't play Daenerys in Game of Thrones because it wasn't really her cup of tea. She didn't like the nudity and didn't like the idea of being famous.

(64) It has been alleged that the reason why HBO replaced Tamzin Merchant as Daenerys is because she didn't have any chemistry with Jason Momoa (who played Khal Drogo).

(65) 90% of the pilot was reshot. Dan Weiss and David Benioff said it just wasn't very good.

(66) Peter Dinklage was not the only person to point out that putting women and children in a crypt during the Battle of Winterfell (in The Long Night) wasn't the smartest move in the world given that the Night King can resurrect the dead!

(67) The Lannisters seem to be fond of Lamprey Pie. Lamprey pie is a traditional dish made with lamprey, a type of jawless fish found in freshwater and saltwater. The lamprey is typically stewed or baked in a pie crust with a variety of seasonings and vegetables. The dish has a rich and savory flavor, and is often enjoyed as a delicacy in certain regions.

(68) Tyrion was a bit nastier in the books. The character had some rough edges smoothed off in the show to take advantage of the likeable and witty performance by Peter Dinklage.

(69) Conleth Hill shaved his head to play Varys. He said he liked this because with his hair grown back he could walk around in complete anonymity.

(70) Jennifer Ehle played Catelyn Stark in the unaired pilot. Michelle Fairley took over this role in the reshoots and series. Jennifer Ehle was not fired but dropped out of her own

accord. Ehle had recently had a baby and decided it was the wrong time to commit to a television show.

(71) Joffrey's death at his own wedding is most likely inspired by Attila the Hun. Attila the Hun died in his sleep in March 453, shortly after celebrating his latest marriage. Some historical accounts suggest that he died from internal bleeding after a night of heavy drinking, while others claim that he succumbed to a nosebleed that he choked on in his sleep. There are also theories that he was murdered by his new wife or members of his own court. Of course, in Game of Thrones we found out why Joffrey died.

(72) In the books, Catelyn Stark is resurrected after her death as Lady Stoneheart and becomes a vengeful and undead figure seeking retribution against those who have wronged her and her family. They decided not to do this in the television show.

(73) It is said that HBO wanted ten seasons of Game of Thrones and George RR Martin felt there was enough material for twelve. Dan Weiss and David Benioff decided to end the show after eight seasons though.

(74) When the eighth season got a poor reception from fans, Dan Weiss and David Benioff copped a lot of criticism for what many saw as a rushed and muddled conclusion to the show.

(75) The reason why Dan Weiss and David Benioff ended Game of Thrones early was apparently to develop a Star Wars film. However, the proposed Star Wars film did not get made in the end.

(76) There was actually a fan petition asking HBO to remake the eighth season of Game of Thrones. This petition obviously stood zero chance of success but it did illustrate how unhappy

some fans had been at season eight.

(77) Dan Weiss and David Benioff have since joked about the bad reception to season eight but one suspects that, deep down, it must have been quite hurtful to them to have the final season prove so controversial and get such a terrible reception.

(78) In the BBC adaptation of I, Claudius, John Hurt gives a memorable performance as the sadistic Caligula (a Roman emperor who ruled from AD 37 to 41). There is definitely something of Caligula in Joffrey Baratheon.

(79) Dan Weiss and David Benioff said the problem with the axed pilot was that it struggled to find the right tone - that balance between drama and fantasy.

(80) The Vale is ruled by House Arryn from the castle of the Eyrie, which is perched atop a mountain and known for its impregnability. The Vale is a mountainous region known for its beautiful landscapes and rich resources.

(81) There was a Sesame Street parody sketch in 2015 called Game of Chairs.

(82) The Red Wedding scenes took about five days to shoot.

(83) In the episode Battle of the Bastards, Lyanna Mormont scowls when Ramsay Bolton claims that he'll pardon the treasonous lords if they take the knee and pledge loyalty. Bella Ramsey said they looked at 60 shots before they got the right scowl!

(84) The wonderful music in Game of Thrones was by Ramin Djawadi. Djawadi's music is known for its epic and cinematic

quality, often incorporating orchestral and electronic elements.

(85) A 2019 poll found that 30% of Americans said they planned to watch the season eight premiere.

(86) George RR Martin said that Sam Tarly was his proxy character - the person he identified with the most. Many of us identify with Sam because he doesn't like violence or war and would much rather spend his time reading in a nice peaceful library!

(87) Over 300 girls auditioned for the part of Arya Stark before they cast Maisie Williams.

(88) The season seven trailer was viewed 61 million times in its first 24 hours.

(89) Isaac Hempstead Wright wears spectacles in real life. Isaac said his bad eyesight was quite useful for adopting the vacant glaze Bran Stark has when he becomes the Raven.

(90) The singer Ed Sheeran famously had a cameo in Game of Thrones as a Lannister soldier. Hodor actor Kristian Nairn was critical of Sheeran's appearance as he felt celebrity cameos took viewers out of the show. Kristian was off the show by then so free to speak his mind!

(91) Ed Sheeran got a lot of pelters for his acting cameo in Game of Thrones but he said he didn't take the criticism too seriously.

(92) The character 'Hot Pie' makes a kidney pie for Brienne and Pod at the crossroads inn. Steak and kidney pie is a traditional British dish that has been around for centuries.

Pies developed in England as a way to preserve meat. If you covered the meat in pastry the food had a longer life.

(93) Anna Popplewell is sometimes alleged to have been on the shortlist to play Daenerys. Popplewell played Susan Pevensie in the fantasy film series The Chronicles of Narnia.

(94) Joffrey Baratheon has parallels with Edward Of Lancaster. Edward's life was cut short at the Battle of Tewkesbury in 1471, where he was killed at the age of 17. His death marked the end of the Lancastrian line. Edward was said to be sadistic and also the product of an illicit affair.

(95) Game of Thrones didn't go in for montages as a rule but there was one in Dragonstone - where we see Sam's tedious (and unpleasant) duties with the chamber pots at the Citadel.

(96) Tom Hollander turned down the part of Littlefinger - which paved the way for Aiden Gillen to take the part. Hollander has been in many things like the Pirates of the Caribbean franchise, Gosford Park, and many television shows. Hollander later said the idea of wearing a 'wolf pelt' in Belfast for half the year wasn't very appealing but if he'd known how big Game of Thrones was going to be he probably wouldn't have turned them down.

(97) Jack Gleeson said that Joaquin Phoenix's Commodus in the film Gladiator was an influence on his portrayal of Joffrey Baratheon.

(98) Emilia Clarke and Lena Headey have something in common outside of Game of Thrones in that they both played Sarah Connor in the Terminator franchise. Emilia Clarke played Conner in the dreadful film Terminator Genisys while Lena Headey fared a bit better playing Connor in the fairly

well liked television show Terminator: The Sarah Connor Chronicles.

(99) The Battle of Agincourt was an influence on the battle in Battle of the Bastards. The Battle of Agincourt was a major English victory during the Hundred Years' War between England and France. The battle took place on October 25, 1415, near the town of Agincourt in northern France. The English army, led by King Henry V, faced off against a much larger French army. Despite being heavily outnumbered, the English were able to secure a decisive victory.

(100) HBO gave season two of Game of Thrones a 15% budget increase.

(101) The Golden Company is a powerful and famed mercenary company in the world of Game of Thrones. They are notorious for their loyalty, discipline, and ruthless efficiency in battle. Originally founded by exiled Westerosi noblemen, the Golden Company has become renowned for their professional and skilled soldiers. Led by their captain, Harry Strickland, the Golden Company is hired by Cersei Lannister to help defend King's Landing against Daenerys Targaryen and her forces.

(102) Brynden Tully is a member of House Tully, a noble family in the Riverlands of Westeros, and is the younger brother of Lord Hoster Tully. He is nicknamed the "Blackfish" for his fierceness and independence. Brynden aids his nephew, Robb Stark, in his bid for the Iron Throne.

(103) Dominic West turned down the part of Mance Rayder because he didn't want to spend six months in Iceland away from his family and was also committed to another project. West said he regretted having to turn Game of Thrones down

and would love to have been in it.

(104) When Sam is slopping out the chamber pots in the Dragonstone montage, the 'slop' in the pots was really wet fruitcake.

(105) Daniel Portman, who played Podrick, is Scottish. He did his audition in both a Scottish and English accent and was then instructed to play Pod with an English accent. Daniel said his own theory is that HBO were worried no one in the United States would be able to understand Scottish accents!

(106) Casterly Rock is the ancestral seat of House Lannister. The castle is built into a rocky cliff, with thick walls and high towers that make it nearly impregnable.

(107) Rory McCann, who played The Hound, is 6'6 tall in real life.

(108) Some of the cast felt the fan petition to remake season eight was disrespectful to all the hard work the crew had gone through to produce the last episodes.

(109) Dan Weiss and David Benioff said the reason the later seasons had fewer episodes is that the budgets were getting so lavish they couldn't afford to have the traditional ten episode run.

(110) Dan Weiss and David Benioff later said they had wanted season eight to consist simply of three feature length episodes but this obviously didn't transpire. The ending would have been even more rushed if this had happened!

(111) Daario Naharis is a flamboyant and skilled warrior who becomes a loyal follower of Daenerys Targaryen. Daario

Naharis was played by Ed Skrein for three episodes before Michiel Huisman took over the role. Ed Skrein, in rather cryptic fashion, said he didn't choose to leave Game of Thrones and it was 'politics' that forced him out.

(112) The recasting of Daario Naharis is quite jarring because Ed Skrein and Michiel Huisman look nothing alike. Michiel Huisman, who is Dutch, is also patently struggling to do an English accent.

(113) A lot of people complained that The Long Night episode was so dark you couldn't see anything!

(114) Tyrion Lannister is rather grotesque looking in the books and loses part of his nose in battle. This was changed in the show as Peter Dinklage is quite handsome and only picks up a scar on his cheek.

(115) Joffrey Baratheon had a pudding bowl haircut in the axed Game of Thrones pilot. This was obviously changed.

(116) Beric Dondarrion was played by David Michael Scott in season one. Richard Dormer took over from season three.

(117) Aside from Northern Ireland, locations for Game of Thrones included Croatia, Spain, and Iceland.

(118) Freddie Stroma was the original actor to play Sam's brother Dickon Tarly. Tom Hopper then took over the part of Dickon. Freddie Stroma did not return due to a scheduling conflict.

(119) Conleth Hill tested fot the part of Robert Baratheon before he was cast as Varys.

(120) Podrick Payne is a squire to Tyrion Lannister and later becomes a squire to Brienne of Tarth. Thanks to his training under Brienne, Podrick becomes quite a skilled swordsman.

(121) Richard Madden and Michelle Fairley knew well in advance that their characters were going to get bumped off at the wedding in The Rains of Castamare. Oona Chaplin also knew that her character Talisa Maegyr was going to be killed too.

(122) Sansa Stark is very partial to lemon cake.

(123) Kerry Ingram had to have screaming lessons to prepare for Shireen Barathon's death scene.

(124) It took about ten hours to film the scene in Battle of the Bastards where Jon smashes Ramsay to the ground with the shield and punches him in the face numerous times.

(125) The original plan in Battle of the Bastards was to see Ramsay Bolton having his jaw ripped off by his own dogs. In the end they sensibly decided this was too graphic and axed that plan.

(126) Struan Rodger was the original Three-Eyed Raven but the much more famous Max Von Sydow later took over this part.

(127) A 2019 poll on Entertainment Weekly ranked The Winds of Winter as the best episode.

(128) Petyr Baelish, also known as Littlefinger, is a cunning and manipulative political schemer who rises from humble beginnings to become a powerful player in the game of thrones. Baelish is known for his ability to manipulate and

deceive others to further his own ambitions, often using his charm and intelligence to outmaneuver his rivals. Baelish makes money by running his own high class brothel in King's Landing.

(129) Mance Rayder is known as the King-Beyond-the-Wall, a title given to the leader of the Free Folk who live beyond the Wall in the north of Westeros. Mance Rayder was a former member of the Night's Watch who deserted and went on to unite the various Free Folk clans under his leadership.

(130) Kerry Ingram, who played Princess Shireen Baratheon, has brittle bone disease so had to be handled with care on the set. Away from Game of Thrones, Kerry has done a lot of musical theatre.

(131) Kristian Nairn, who played Hodor, is 6'10 in height.

(132) Dame Diana Rigg said she had no idea that Game of Thrones was such a big show when she signed up to play Lady Olenna Tyrell.

(133) Kit Harington said it was quite common for them to shoot 'fake' scenes on Game of Thrones as a misdirection device aimed at preventing spoilers.

(134) Dean-Charles Chapman said that when he signed to play Tommen Baratheon he had no idea that the character was going to become the king and he also had no idea the character was going to die.

(135) Jaime Lannister is the eldest son of Tywin Lannister, Jaime is known as the Kingslayer for his role in assassinating King Aerys II. Jamie is in a relationship with his sister Cersei and the real father of her children. This fact seems to be an

open secret - though the Lannisters do their best to deny it.

(136) A 2019 poll on Entertainment Weekly ranked Oberyn Martell's demise at the hands of the Mountain as the most 'epic' death in the show.

(137) Alexander Siddig, who played Prince Doran, said there was supposed to be a long complex arc for his character and Dorne (as in the books) but they never did any of this in the end.

(138) Mahershala Ali unsuccessfully auditioned for the part of Xaro Xhoan Daxos.

(139) Charlie Hunnam was supposed to appear as Rhaegar Targaryen but he couldn't do it in the end because he was too busy.

(140) Peter Dinklage as Tyrion appeared in more episodes than anyone else.

(141) Winterfell is the ancestral seat of House Stark. The castle is located in the northern region of Westeros and serves as the seat of the rulers of the North.

(142) It is often reported that, despite being in it, Bella Ramsey wasn't allowed to watch Game of Thrones on television due to still being a kid. Bella said this is not exactly true and that they had watched a few bits of the show before.

(143) Isaac Hempstead Wright was only ten years old when he started playing Bran Stark.

(144) After they shot the pilot, Sophie Turner and Maisie Williams both assumed the show would not be picked up and

they'd never play these characters again.

(145) Khal Drogo was a Dothraki warlord who was married to Daenerys Targaryen.

(146) The food the men of the Night's Watch have to eat is notoriously bad. Their staple diet seems to be stew with tough meat.

(147) Having not really watched much of the show, Bella Ramsey didn't have the faintest clue what was going in the plot and her scenes! Bella just turned up and did the lines.

(149) Dean-Charles Chapman played Martyn Lannister in two episodes before taking the role of Tommen Baratheon.

(150) The pond at Winterfell was filled with black paint to make it look mystical and reflective.

(151) Aimee Richardson was the original Myrcella Baratheon but replaced by Nell Tiger Free later on.

(152) Season five of the show caught up with the books and then had to plough its own furrow (so to speak). There is sometimes a perception that Dan Weiss and David Benioff were good at adapting material but not so good at coming up with it themselves. The real picture is more complex because there were certainly some good episodes after the loss of the source material. George RR Martin said it is best to think of the books and the show as distinct from one another. They are not the same thing and differ in numerous aspects.

(153) Iwan Rheon auditioned to play Jon Snow before he was cast as Ramsay Bolton. Iwan was best known to British audiences at the time for his role in the cultish superhero

show Misfits.

(154) Tom McCarthy directed the unused Game of Thrones pilot. McCarthy was probably best known at the time directing the film The Station Agent with Peter Dinklage. For the reshoots, McCarthy was replaced with Tim Van Patten. Van Patten was an experienced television director who had worked on shows like The Sopranos, Deadwood, and Rome.

(155) The famous episode Blackwater cost $8 million to make.

(156) According to a poll, 36% of Americans said they disliked the last ever episode. Bad writing was the most common complaint for why they didn't like it.

(157) Fifty-nine characters died in the first season.

(158) Maisie Williams said she would happily play Arya Stark again in a spin-off show if the chance ever arose.

(159) Izzy Meikle-Small was the main rival to Sophie Turner for the part of Sansa Stark and in the end it came down to a choice between these two. Izzy Meikle-Small is an English actress who has appeared in (among other things) Outlander and Ripper Street.

(160) The late Ray Stevenson, who starred in HBO's Rome and many other things, said he turned down a part of Game of Thrones in the third season. He did not specify which part he turned down. Rather than appear in Game of Thrones he instead took a part in Black Sails.

(161) Nicholas Hoult revealed in 2019 that he unsuccessfully auditioned for the part of Jon Snow.

(162) A number of fans felt that the character of Euron Greyjoy was nowhere near as complex and vivid in the show as he was in the books. Pilou Asbæk, who played Euron in the show, also felt this way.

(163) Emilia Clarke suffered two brain hemorrhages while still in her twenties. She said she is lucky to be alive.

(164) Danny Dyer said he was rejected three times by Game of Thrones. Dyer said he tested to play Pypar. It was Josef Altin who bagged this part in the show.

(165) Ned Stark is described as plain looking in the books. In the show though he is played by the ruggedly handsome Sean Bean.

(166) Peter Dinklage was the only actor George RR Martin and the producers wanted for Tyrion Lannister. Thankfully they managed to get him.

(167) Mead is an alcoholic beverage made by fermenting honey with water. It is often referred to as honey wine.

(168) The arrival of Brienne and Pod to save Sansa and Theon from the Bolton soldiers in The Red Woman is desperately welcome and needed because Sansa and Theon's plight was so grim we almost couldn't take anymore. Brienne taking out the soldiers (with help from Pod) is incredibly satisfying.

(169) Coldplay drummer Will Champion had a cameo in the Red Wedding episode.

(170) Edmure Tully is depicted as somewhat incompetent in the television show - which was not the case in the books.

(171) Mark Gatiss has a small part in Game of Thrones as Tycho Nestoris - a representative of the Iron Bank of Braavos. Gatiss is an actor and writer best known for playing Mycroft Holmes in the BBC show Sherlock. He is also well known in Britain for being part of the comedy team The League of Gentlemen.

(172) Jaqen H'ghar is a mysterious assassin who is part of a group of skilled killers known as the Faceless Men. Jaqen is known for his ability to change his appearance at will and for his lethal skills in combat. He talks in puzzles and eventually trains Ayra.

(173) Patrick Malahide, who played Balon Greyjoy, is a very distinguished actor with a long CV. He said though that he got more public recognition for Game of Thrones than anything else he has ever done. Malahide, before Thrones, was probably best known to British audiences as the sarcastic Detective Sergeant Chisholm in the popular 80s show Minder.

(174) Theon Greyjoy is the youngest son of Lord Balon Greyjoy of the Iron Islands, an independent kingdom off the west coast of Westeros. Theon is taken as a hostage and ward by Lord Eddard Stark of Winterfell following a failed rebellion by the Greyjoys. He grows up at Winterfell alongside his captor's children, Jon Snow and Robb Stark, but always feels like an outsider and struggles with his identity. In his quest to prove himself to his family, Theon makes a series of decisions that ultimately lead to his downfall. He betrays the Starks and takes Winterfell by force, but is eventually captured and tortured by Ramsay Bolton, a sadistic psychopath who forces him to assume the identity of "Reek." Theon eventually finds redemption through helping Sansa Stark escape from Winterfell and returning to the Iron Islands to support his sister Yara in her bid for power.

(175) The Dothraki are a nomadic horse-riding tribe known for their fierce warrior culture, adherence to tradition and their skilled cavalry units. Their society is organised into clans, with a strict hierarchy and customs that revolve around strength, honour, and loyalty.

(176) In 2017 it was reported that 11 baby boys in England had been given the name Tyrion in tribute to Game of Thrones.

(177) Gwendoline Christie put on a stone in muscle mass through workouts to play Brienne of Tarth.

(178) Kristian Nairn, who played Hodor, said he ended up with back trouble because of all the scenes where he has to carry Bran around!

(179) Maester Luwin is the maester at Winterfell at the start of the show. He serves as a trusted advisor to the Stark family. Maester Luwin is known for his wisdom, intelligence, and loyalty to House Stark. He plays a pivotal role in guiding and educating the Stark children.

(180) Game of Thrones was the patent inspiration for a slew of medieval/historical action dramas. The most successful of these were Vikings, The Last Kingdom, and Black Sails.

(181) After Ned's death, Arya poses as a boy with a short haircut. Maisie Williams actually cut her hair off herself.

(182) Alfie Allen died his blonde hair brown to play Theon.

(183) Daenerys is supposed to be seventeen at the start of the show. Emilia Clarke was 23 in real ife. Daenerys is about fourteen in the first book.

(184) Sophie Turner said she found it difficult to cope with the fame that came from being in Game of thrones.

(185) Lino Facioli, who played the erratic and pampered Lord Robin Arryn, was born in Brazil and moved to Britain when he was four. Since the end of Game of Thrones, Lino has been in Sex Education and Masters of the Air.

(186) The Battle of Winterfell episode with the White Walkers was shot near Belfast in freezing conditions.

(187) Bella Ramsey first learned of being cast in Game of Thrones after coming home from school in the afternoon.

(188) The Dorne escapades in season five and the 'Sand Snakes' are often held up as one of the worst plot tangents.

(189) The Unsullied is a group of warrior-eunuchs known for their incredible discipline and skill in battle. Trained from a young age to be fierce and fearless soldiers, the Unsullied are considered some of the best fighters in the world of Westeros. Led by their commander Grey Worm, the Unsullied are loyal to their queen, Daenerys Targaryen.

(190) The show's production used over 3,000 visual effects shots in the final season.

(191) Finn Jones, who played Loras Tyrell, also auditioned for the parts of Jon Snow and Robb Stark.

(192) After being cast in Game of Thrones, Bella Ramsey had to keep it secret for an entire year.

(193) Maesters are trained in various subjects such as science, history, and medicine, and serve as advisors, scholars, and

healers to the noble families of Westeros. They are members of the Order of Maesters and are known for wearing chains of different metals that represent their areas of expertise.

(194) Emilia Clarke later had four different wigs on rotation to play Daenerys. There are a few wig continuity bloopers in the show where you see the hair of Daenerys change in the middle of a scene.

(195) Tyrion and Cersei might loathe each other but Peter Dinklage and Lena Headey are friends and would often drive to the set together.

(196) In the scene where Daenerys has to eat a horse heart, Emilia Clarke was really eating a big piece of solidified jam covered in fake blood. Emilia said the jam wasn't very nice - though of course preferable to eating a heart!

(197) Nikolaj Coster-Waldau is actually Danish in real life but he does a pretty good English accent as Jamie.

(198) The famous 'Red Wedding' sequence in Game of Thrones was based on the Black Dinner of 1440. The Black Dinner of 1440 was a historic event that took place in Edinburgh. The dinner was hosted by King James II of Scotland and included two rival clans, the Douglas and the Livingston. The dinner ended in tragedy when the king ordered the execution of the Douglas brothers, who were the leaders of their clan.

(199) Ian McElhinney was unhappy that his character Ser Barristan Selmy was to be killed off and asked the showrunners if they might reconsider this. Dan Weiss and David Benioff later joked that McElhinney's request made them even more determined to bump off Ser Barristan. Suffice to say, this incident did little to endear Weiss and

Benioff to fans.

(200) Rory McCann, who played the Hound, said there were no 'divas' in the Game of Thrones cast and everyone was nice to work with.

(201) It is all down to personal taste, but many consider the first four seasons of the show to be the best. Season six is also highly rated.

(202) Season eight had the most deaths. Over 3,000 people perished in this season.

(203) A lot was lost from the books in the television adaptation. Because the books are so dense and complex and have so many characters and arcs it would have been nigh on impossible to do a completely faithful adaptation - not unless the show ran for twenty five seasons.

(204) Maisie Williams said she was always excited when she got a costume change as Arya because it didn't happen that often.

(205) George RR Martin said that Littlefinger was the character who changed the most in the book to television adaptation.

(206) The burn marks on the Hound's face are more elaborate and gruesome in the books than the television show.

(207) Game of Thrones used drones and security guards to keep their filming private. There were many incidents of people trying to sneak into the locations.

(208) The land north of the wall in Game of Thrones is a vast

area bigger than the United States.

(209) The little direwolves used in the show are actually Northern Inuit dogs, a breed known for their wolf-like appearance.

(210) Margaret John, who Played Old Nan, died during the shooting of season one. Out of respect the part was not recast.

(211) George RR Martin was a consultant on the television show but said he had little power over the stories and content. They could basically do what they whatever wanted in the show.

(212) Natalie Dormer was already a fan of Game of Thrones when she joined the show.

(213) Nikolaj Coster-Waldau has been candid about the fact he argued with the showrunners over Jamie sticking with Cersei to the bitter end - despite everything she had done.

(214) Natalia Tena, who played Osha, is the lead singer of a band called Molotov Jukebox

(215) Tormund Giantsbane is a fierce and loyal Wildling warrior, known for his humour, bravery, and distinctive red hair and beard. Tormund forms a close friendship with Jon Snow.

(216) Lyanna Mormont's death scene was so complex to shoot that Bella Ramsey was later called back to the set five times to do more work on it.

(217) Nina Gold was the casting director on Game of Thrones. Nina said it was especially tough finding the right children to

play the Stark kids.

(218) A number of cast members said that wearing armour in the show was uncomfortable and not very pleasant.

(219) Davos Seaworth is a loyal advisor to Stannis Baratheon early in the show. Davos is known for his diplomacy skills and is also an experienced sailor. He later becomes the advisor to Jon Snow.

(220) Tricia Helfer said on Twitter that she tested for the part of Cersei. Helfer is best known for playing Number Six in the (rebooted) science fiction series Battlestar Galactica.

(221) Emilia Clarke is a brunette in real life.

(222) Season four of Game of Thrones is the highest rated season of the show on Rotten Tomatoes.

(223) Emilia Clarke is only 5'2.

(224) A 2019 poll on Entertainment Weekly ranked season six as the best season.

(225) One of the influences on the battle sequences in Battle of the Bastards was the Battle of Cannae. The Battle of Cannae was a major battle fought during the Second Punic War between the Roman Republic and the Carthaginian Empire in 216 BC. The Carthaginian army, led by the legendary general Hannibal, decisively defeated the larger Roman army, led by Consuls Gaius Terentius Varro and Lucius Aemilius Paullus. Hannibal employed a brilliant strategy that utilised his superior cavalry and infantry forces to encircle and trap the Roman army, resulting in a devastating defeat for the Romans.

(226) The Night King was played by two different actors - Richard Brake and Vladimir Furdik. Brake's departure is presumed to have been that that old acting chestnut - scheduling problems. Vladimir Furdik was already a stunt performer on the show.

(227) Balon Greyjoy is the head of House Greyjoy and the lord of the Iron Islands, a group of rocky islands off the western coast of Westeros. Balon is a fiercely independent and ambitious leader.

(228) The directors and producers on Game of Thrones said it was a bit intimidating working with Dame Diana Rigg.

(229) The show's dragons, Drogon, Rhaegal, and Viserion, were brought to life using a combination of practical and CGI effects.

(230) Kit Harington broke his leg during season three so they had to use body doubles in some of the Jon Snow scenes.

(231) Bronn is a skilled fighter and sellsword in Game of Thrones. He is a mercenary and is known for his sharp wit and cunning tactics in a fight. Bronn forms a bond with Tyrion Lannister and Jaime Lannister - who both employ Bronn.

(232) Lena Headey said she was disappointed that there was not a Daenerys/Cersei scene in the last season.

(233) Sansa Stark is is initially portrayed as a shallow and selfish young girl. Sansa becomes a strong and resilient leader after enduring years of abuse and manipulation. She eventually rises to become the Queen of the North.

(234) Callum Wharry played the young Tommen Baratheon

before Dean-Charles Chapman took over the role.

(235) Bran Stark is the youngest son of Eddard Stark. Bran becomes the Three-Eyed Raven after a near-fatal fall leaves him paralysed. With the ability to see into the past, present, and future, Bran plays a crucial role in the battle against the Night King and the White Walkers.

(236) Battle of the Bastards is unusual for Game of Thrones because there are a few slow motion scenes.

(237) It rained heavily while they were filming the battle scene in Battle of the Bastards. The cast and extras got very wet and muddy.

(238) Cersei Lannister is the ambitious and ruthless Queen of the Seven Kingdoms. Cersei will stop at nothing to maintain her grip on power.

(239) Joffrey mentions Ser Duncan the Tall in Two Swords. This is a character from George RR Martin's Dunk and Egg trilogy - which is set to become another prequel television show.

(240) Initially, the Battle of the Blackwater was going to happen offscreen but thankfully they managed to find the money to stage it in the end.

(241) Missandei is much younger in the books and just a child.

(242) The Iron Throne in the books is much bigger than the one in the show.

(243) Dean-Charles Chapman made his first appearance as Tommen Baratheon in The Lion and the Rose.

(244) One of the things that makes Jack Gleeson's Joffrey so annoying and a great villain is that even his voice grates! Gleeson deliberately makes Joffrey's voice sneering and whiney.

(245) The sigil of House Tyrell is a rose.

(246) Waymar Royce is the first character in the show to be killed.

(247) House Martell's sigil is a red sun and a golden spear.

(248) Ian McShane made a guest appearance in one episode of Game of Thrones as Brother Ray. McShane's distaste for a burger he was served at lunch while on the show apparently made the production change their caterers!

(249) The sigil of House Baratheon is a stag.

(250) President Obama was allowed to view the season four premiere before it was released.

(251) Olly, the orphan boy who is taken in by the Night's Watch, was an invention of the television show and not in the books.

(252) Jack Gleeson said he enjoyed the scene of the late Joffrey lying in state because he could have a snooze!

(253) In the episode Blackwater, Tyrion is cut in the face during the battle. The wound was done using CGI.

(254) The showrunners wanted a storyline where Davos develops a crush on Missandei but Liam Cunningham refused to do it. He felt the storyline was inappropriate and distasteful

given that he was nearly thirty years older than Nathalie Emmanuel. He felt it was out of character for Davos - who was a father figure to Shireen.

(255) When they made the episode Blackwater, there was only one big replica ship for the production so they simply used CGI to recreate this ship and give the appearance of a fleet.

(256) Jorah's father in Game of Thrones is played by James Cosmo. In real life though Cosmo is only about twelve years older than Jorah actor Iain Glen.

(257) The Hound is very fond of ale. Ale is a type of beer that is typically brewed with a higher amount of hops and a longer fermentation process, resulting in a more complex taste.

(258) Gemma Whelan played the niece of Euron Greyjoy in the show. In real life though, Pilou Asbæk, the actor who played Euron, is younger than Gemma Whelan.

(259) Peter Dinklage as Tyrion has the most lines out of anyone in the cast.

(260) Sansa is supposed to be thirteen in season one.

(261) Sean Bean as Ned Stark has more lines than anyone else in season one.

(262) Jerome Flynn was famous for his blonde hair when he was younger. It was dyed black to play Bronn.

(263) Season six is the first season where Kit Harington as Jon Snow has the most lines.

(264) Before the seventh season of Game of Thrones came out,

Harry Potter star Daniel Radcliffe said he'd love to be in the show and get a gruesome death!

(265) A 2024 Esquire article ranked Cersei Lannister as the most interesting and complex character in the show.

(266) Season eight went into production with the secret codename Face of Angels.

(267) When we first meet Jaqen H'Ghar he is in Westeros. It is never really explained though why he is there.

(268) Eddison Tollett is nicknamed Dolorous Edd in the books. There is a mention of this nickname in the television series.

(269) Illyrio Mopatis is the person who arranges the wedding of Daenerys Targaryen and Khal Drogo and gifts her three dragon eggs. This character disappeared after two episodes - which is a shame as the actor Roger Allam was terrific.

(270) Sandor Clegane is supposed to be the younger brother of Gregor Clegane. In real life though Rory McCann is nearly twenty years older than (the last Gregor actor) Hafþór Júlíus Björnsson

(271) Tyrion has different coloured eyes in the books. They didn't do this in the television show because Peter Dinklage would have had to wear a contact lens in every scene.

(272) When we see Jon Snow lying on a slab before he is resurrected by the Red Woman, Kit Harington said he fell asleep a few times.

(273) Dan Weiss and David Benioff have largely maintained a radio silence on Game of Thrones since it ended. They did

though talk about it a bit when they promoted their Netflix show 3 Body Problem. Benioff admitted that not everyone liked season eight of Thrones.

(274) Rory McCann did a commercial for the breakfast cereal Scott's Porridge Oats in the 1990s where he was bathing in a lake.

(275) Kit Harington's Jon Snow costume got so elaborate in the end it weighed 33 pounds.

(276) A large number of actors have appeared in both Game of Thrones and Doctor Who. Maisie Williams, David Bradley, Joe Dempsie, Lucian Msamati, Harry Lloyd, Mark Gatiss, Paul Kaye and many others.

(277) When the show ended, the Game of Thrones producers gave cast members storyboards and special gifts as props.

(278) During the Changing of the Guard at Buckingham Palace in 2014, the Queen's guards performed the Game of Thrones theme.

(279) Sophie Turner took home one of Sansa's corsets as a momento when the show ended.

(280) Theon apparently became quite a popular baby name when Game of Thrones was on.

(281) George Lucas visited the Game of Thrones set when they were shooting the first episode of season eight.

(282) Jerome Flynn said he loved playing Bronn and would be up for the character appearing in a spin-off show.

(283) Kit Harington had a black eye when he auditioned for Game of Thrones because he had an altercation with a man who was rude to his girlfriend in a fast food place.

(284) The Red Woman is the first episode where we see that Podrick, under Brienne's training, has become quite a handy swordsman.

(285) In the episode Blackwater, we see the Hound cut a man in half on the battlefield. This was a practical effect done with a dummy.

(286) Joe Dempsie, who played Gendry, said that when Game of Thrones ended it felt a bit like leaving school.

(287) According to data by Spin Genie, Game of Thrones is the most popular television show in history when you factor in viewers, social media interest, media articles etc. Stranger Things ranked second.

(288) It took two months to create the Iron Throne seen in the show.

(289) Viserys Targaryen mentions a dragon named Vermithrax in the first season. This is the name of a dragon in the 1981 film Dragonslayer.

(290) George RR Martin is a big fan of the film Dragonslayer. The character named Tyrian in the film most likely inspired Tyrion Lannister's name.

(291) Nikolaj Coster-Waldau's wife is a former Miss Greenland.

(292) The memorable title sequence in Game of Thrones actually won an Emmy.

(293) Peter Dinklage said he turns down fantasy roles that are similar to Game of Thrones because he would prefer to do something different.

(294) Gwendoline Christie gave up alcohol and took up kick boxing to get in the best possible shape to play Brienne.

(295) Qyburn is a former maester of the Citadel who was expelled for conducting forbidden experiments. Qyburn becomes a loyal ally to Cersei Lannister and serves as her Master of Whisperers and Hand of the Queen. He is known for his dark and manipulative nature, using his knowledge of science and medicine to further Cersei's goals.

(296) The makers of the Netflix show Stranger Things consulted with the Game of Thrones producers on how to keep their sets private and avoid spoilers leaking in the press.

(297) The 'dragons' on the set were just a pole with a ball attached - which the actors had to look at, react to, and pretend was a dragon. The dragons were obviously added in later with digital special effects.

(298) Peter Dinklage said the main difference between him and Tyrion is that he's quite shy in real life whereas Tyrion is very confident.

(299) The second season of Game of Thrones was ordered by HBO just a few days after the premiere of the first episode.

(300) Nikolaj Coster-Waldau said the Game of Thrones cast have a chat group and stay in touch.

(301) The final season of Game of Thrones famously featured a coffee cup accidentally left in one of the scenes. It was

removed by HBO on their streaming platform once they noticed the gaffe.

(302) Bella Ramsey said they had no idea if people would like Lyanna Mormont in Game of Thrones. It turned out that they DID. Lyanna Mormont was very popular.

(303) Game of Thrones is one of the most pirated television shows in history.

(304) Kit Harington became a very skilled horse rider through Game of Thrones.

(305) Esmé Bianco, who played the prostitute Ros, is also a Neo-burlesque performer.

(306) Jorah Mormont is a former knight and exiled lord of House Mormont who serves as an advisor and loyal protector to Daenerys Targaryen. Jorah is known for his loyalty, bravery, and unrequited love for Daenerys.

(307) Melisandre is a Red Priestess of the Lord of Light, a powerful and enigmatic figure who uses her magic and influence to further her own interests and support the cause of Stannis Baratheon.

(308) Bella Ramsey has expressed gratitude towards Game of Thrones for providing the opportunity to launch an acting career.

(309) The Iron Bank in Braavos is a powerful financial institution in the world of Game of Thrones, known for its strict repayment policies and willingness to fund various factions and individuals in the pursuit of power.

(310) Sam Coleman played the young Hodor in two episodes. Sam later had a part in the horror film Leatherface.

(311) Rory McCann said that playing the Hound in Game of Thrones was the best role he'll ever have.

(312) In the season three scene where the Hound and Arya arrive at the Eryie and Arya laughs when she learns her aunt has died, Maisie Williams watched funny videos on her phone to make her laugh genuine!

(313) Because the show had such a big cast spread across different locations, there were cast members who only ever met each other at press events and script readings.

(314) Maisie Williams said that Rory McCann was a lot like his character the Hound because he got grumpy if he hadn't had any food!

(315) Peter Dinklage said he doesn't mind if people only think of him as Tyrion Lannister because that would at least be evidence he created a memorable character.

(316) The Hundred Years' War was an influence on the books and story in Game of Thrones. The Hundred Years' War was a series of conflicts fought between England and France from 1337 to 1453. The war was primarily fought over disputes over the control of the French throne and territories in France controlled by the English monarchy.

(317) Lysa Arryn is the sister of Catelyn Stark and the wife of the late Jon Arryn, the former Hand of the King. Lysa is known for her paranoia, overprotectiveness of her son Robin, and her intense love for Petyr Baelish, whom she marries after Jon Arryn's death.

(318) Lady Olenna was the matriarch of House Tyrell and known for her sharp wit, cunning political savvy, and fierce loyalty to her family. She was also known as the Queen of Thorns for her sharp tongue and ability to outmaneuver her enemies.

(319) Arya Stark is the youngest daughter of House Stark. Arya seeks revenge for the deaths of her family members. Trained as an assassin by the Faceless Men, she uses her skills to eliminate her enemies and protect her loved ones.

(320) Tyrion Lannister is the witty and intelligent younger brother of Cersei and Jaime Lannister. He might be small but he has the biggest heart of all the Lannisters. Tyrion is the most human and decent of the Lannister clan.

(321) Pedro Pascal said it was easy to come into Game of Thrones because the cast were so friendly it was like one big family.

(322) Lyanna Mormont is the cousin of Ser Jorah Mormont.

(323) Daenerys Targaryen is the last surviving member of House Targaryen - or so she thinks. Daenerys is known as the Mother of Dragons.

(324) The sigil of House Stark is a grey direwolf on a white field.

(325) A lot of the cast were later fairly open about their view that the show declined in quality in the last few seasons.

(326) Bella Ramsey had to go to Manchester to do the audition for Game of Thrones. Bella was given a script to learn before the audition.

(327) Game of Thrones aired for 8 seasons, consisting of a total of 73 episodes.

(328) Throughout the show's eight seasons, approximately 186 named characters in Game of Thrones were killed off.

(329) Kit Harington was 23 years old when he was cast in the show.

(330) Led Zeppelin singer Robert Plant said he turned down a cameo in Game of Thrones.

(331) In the books the White Walkers are known as the 'Others' but they dropped this in the television adaptation because the 'Others' was a common phrase in the TV show Lost.

(332) Gendry is younger in the books than he was in the television show.

(333) King's Landing often tops polls of fictional places where people would most like to visit.

(334) Oded Fehr was considered for the part of Oberyn played by Pedro Pascal. Oded Fehr was in the Mummy films with Brendan Fraser.

(335) John Bradley was late for his Game of Thrones audition because his train was cancelled. Happily though he still got the part of Sam.

(336) Sophie Turner said the wine you see characters drinking in Game of Thrones was really grape juice. She said it was revolting!

(337) Joffrey's death wasn't deemed gruesome enough so Jack Gleeson later had to go Los Angeles to film a few extra insert shots.

(338) Kit Harington said he was lumbered with a terrible wig in the abandoned pilot.

(339) The director on Bella Ramsey's first Games of Thrones episode said Bella was already word perfect and brilliant.

(340) Some of the extras who played Wildings in the show said they wore jeans under the fake furs!

(341) Before the development of House of the Dragon, HBO did a pilot for a prequel show called Bloodmoon. The pilot's cast included Naomi Watts and Jamie Campbell Bower and was set 1,000 years before Game of Thrones. The story was allegedly about the first conflict with the White Walkers and the building of the Wall.

(342) HBO spent $30 million on the Bloodmoon pilot but decided not to go ahead with a series. The pilot has never been seen. HBO said the pilot did not 'gel' and felt it wasn't strong enough to be a show. It was written by Jane Goldman and an original story not based on any books.

(343) Bloodman was designed to be very different to Game of Thrones and was described as very ambitious. In the end though HBO obviously got cold feet and decided to pivot away to the slow burn political intrigue of House of the Dragon.

(344) The Wildings have some obvious parallels to the Vikings.

(345) Memory, Sorrow, and Thorn by Tad Williams was an influence on George RR Martin writing the books. Memory,

Sorrow, and Thorn is a high fantasy series consisting of three books: The Dragonbone Chair, Stone of Farewell, and To Green Angel Tower. The series follows the story of a young man named Simon who embarks on an epic quest to save his kingdom from a powerful evil force known as the Storm King.

(346) Carice van Houten said Sam Tarly was her favourite character.

(347) Game of Thrones was the first acting audition that John Bradley ever did.

(348) Valyrian Steel is known for being incredibly sharp, strong, and valuable. Valyrian Steel is said to be forged with spells and dragonfire in the ancient city of Valyria, and it is extremely rare in the world of Westeros. Swords made of Valyrian Steel are highly sought after and often passed down through noble families for generations. Valyrian Steel is one of the few substances that can kill White Walkers.

(349) Qarth is a wealthy trading port located in the southern part of Essos.

(350) Milk of the poppy is basically morphine.

(351) Carice van Houten said she was shocked when she saw the fate of Shireen Baratheon in the script.

(352) The men of the Night's Watch are not allowed to marry or have a family.

(353) Greyscale is an infectious disease that causes the skin to turn into scales and stone - or something much like it. The condition need not be fatal though as Shireen and Jorah survived it.

(354) Gemma Whelan's background was in comedy and so she enjoyed sinking her acting chops into the more dramatic role of Yara Greyjoy.

(355) Isaac Hempstead Wright said that, despite what he did to Bran, Jamie Lannister was actually his favourite character.

(356) The first episode (Winter is Coming) is the only time we see the Stark family all together.

(357) Pedro Pascal said that filming Oberyn's fight with the Mountain was a lot of fun.

(358) Kit Harington said he did his Jon Snow audition in his normal accent but was asked to impersonate Sean Bean's Yorkshire accent on the show.

(359) George RR Martin said in 2022 that he was left 'out of the loop' on the last two seasons of Game of Thrones.

(360) Iwan Rheon said he based the cocky swagger of Ramsay Bolton on the pop star Liam Gallagher!

(361) Aerys II Targaryen, the 'mad king', has some parallels with Ivan the Terrible. Ivan IV Vasilyevich, commonly known as Ivan the Terrible, was the Tsar of Russia from 1547 to 1584. He is remembered as a ruthless and tyrannical leader who instigated the oprichnina, a period of mass repression and terror in Russia. Ivan's reign was marked by numerous acts of violence and cruelty, including the infamous massacre of Novgorod in 1570.

(362) Robert E. Howard was a big influence on George RR Martin. Robert E. Howard (1906-1936) was an American author best known for creating the character Conan the

Barbarian. Howard is considered one of the pioneers of the sword and sorcery genre of fiction, and his work has had a major influence on the fantasy genre as a whole.

(363) The extras on the show who played Night Watch members and Wildings said Kit Harington was a very humble and nice man who would often go to the pub with them.

(364) The Long Night episode required 800 extras.

(365) Rory McCann played Lurch in the 2007 comedy film Hot Fuzz. Hodor actor Kristian Nairn went up for this part too.

(366) Lyanna Mormont's blunt manner of speaking, often delivering scathing verbal takedowns, made the character instantly cultish.

(367) Pedro Pascal said the first scene he shot for Game of Thrones was when Prince Oberyn visits Tyrion in the dungeon and offers to be his champion in the trial by combat.

(368) In 2019 it was estimated that HBO had made at least a couple of billion from Game of Thrones merchandise.

(369) Maisie Williams said doing fight scenes with swords was the most difficult thing to do on Game of Thrones.

(370) Bella Ramsey said that their aunt was a bit disturbed by Lyanna Mormont's death scene in Game of Thrones!

(371) Sophie Turner said (in her opinion) she wasn't very good as Sansa early in the show but felt her acting got better as the show progressed because she was surrounded by so many good actors.

(372) Oberyn Martell is known as the Red Viper of Dorne.

(373) Robert Aramayo played the young Ned Stark in four episodes. Robert was later in The Lord of the Rings: The Rings of Power. Sebastian Croft played an even younger version of Ned in two episodes.

(374) Jermome Flynn said he was a bit dubious about whether Game of Thrones would work because HBO were essentially doing (on a bigger budget) a British style medieval show and he wondered if they would be able to get the tone and drama right. As it turned out HBO did a terrific job and Jerome's fears were soon banished.

(375) The scrapped pilot opened with a scene of Jon Arryn dying of poison.

(376) George RR Martin said he was angered by the backlash to season eight.

(377) Lena Headey was pregnant when she filmed the first episode (or second pilot if you prefer). They had to hide this with furs or have her sit down a lot.

(378) Ian McNeice played Illyrio Mopatis in the scrapped pilot. Roger Allam replaced him in the series.

(379) Blackwater was the most expensive episode of the series at the time of its airing.

(380) Game of Thrones became a cultural phenomenon, with fans around the world hosting viewing parties.

(381) The show's production used over 1,000 costumes per season.

(382) Lord Varys is a eunuch and the Master of Whisperers on the Small Council in King's Landing. He is known for his intelligence, strategic thinking, and ability to gather information through his vast network of "little birds."

(383) Kit Harington was not permitted to cut his hair short while Game of Thrones was in production.

(384) They spent two months designing and testing different wigs for the character of Deanerys.

(385) Richard Madden has joked that after playing Robb Stark he rarely gets invited to weddings!

(386) Jon Snow was raised as the bastard son of Eddard Stark. Jon joins the Night's Watch and rises through the ranks to become Lord Commander. He later learns of his true heritage as the son of Rhaegar Targaryen and Lyanna Stark, making him a legitimate contender for the Iron Throne.

(387) Pedro Pascal based Oberyn's accent on his father's accent. Pedro's father was from Chile.

(388) Iwan Rheon said that after shooting the scene where Ramsay Bolton is eaten by his own dogs as Sansa watches, he went for a drink with Sophie Turner to mark his end on the show.

(389) Game of Thrones was only the second acting audition that Maisie Williams had ever done.

(390) Peter Dinklage said he liked the fact that Tyrion was neither a hero nor a villain and a flawed person.

(391) Before season three, Maisie Williams was asked who she

would like to end up on the Iron Throne. She suggested Bronn because then the people would have a funny king!

(392) John Bradley said he was thrilled when he got to do a scene with Stephen Dillane as Stannis because Stephen Dillane is one of his favourite actors.

(393) Rory McCann said it was so cold in Iceland that the sweat under his prosthetic Hound facial makeup would turn into ice.

(394) Joe Dempsie and Bella Ramsey both started acting through the Nottingham Television Workshop.

(395) Kit Harington is only 5'8 tall.

(396) Bella Ramsey said that Game of Thrones was sort of like their version of acting school.

(397) Game of Thrones was hard work because they would shoot the same scene many times over using different camera angles and camera lenses.

(398) We don't see the Battle of the Green Fork in Baelor because the producers didn't have enough money to stage it.

(399) There are some amusing references to Monty Python and the Holy Grail in Breaker of Chains.

(400) The sigil of House Tully is a silver trout emerging over waves.

(401) Maisie Williams said it wasn't true that the coffee cup left in a season eight scene was a Starbucks coffee cup. She said it was just a cup. At the time you couldn't get Starbucks

in Belfast.

(402) The Iron Throne in the show is over eight feet tall.

(403) Nikolaj Coster-Waldau said a particular highlight of the show for him was Dame Diana Rigg's last scene because it was just Diana and him in the scene.

(404) Bella Ramsey said their worst moment on Game of Thrones was when they ruined a take by getting Lyanna Mormont's cloak snagged on a bench!

(405) In a 2013 Daily Mail interview, Gillian Anderson seemed to suggest she turned down Game of Thrones. She did not specify which part she turned down but it is often presumed to be Cersei Lannister.

(406) Kit Harington's real name is Christopher Catesby Harington. Kit is a childhood nickname.

(407) Bella Ramsey didn't do many interviews for Game of Thrones due to being so young.

(408) The battle sequence in Battle of the Bastards was ground level not just to make it more visceral but also because overhead drones and cameras would have scared the horses.

(409) Jamie Lannister's fake hand was solid gold in the books.

(410) Charles Dance hadn't read the books and learned the fate of Tywin from an autograph hunter.

(411) Davos Seaworth is a 'window' character for the audience because he is kind and low-born. We can identify with Davos.

(412) David Benioff & Dan Weiss said they decided not to have Jon Snow kill the Night King because it would be too obvious and predictable.

(413) Eugene Simon, who played Lancel Lannister, also auditioned for the part of Joffrey Baratheon.

(414) Sean Bean said his favourite character in the show was Varys.

(415) The inevitable fight between the brothers Gregor and Sandor is known as Clegane Bowl.

(416) Rory McCann said he loved the road trip that the Hound takes with Arya because he enjoyed working with Maisie Williams and it was lovely to be outside a lot rather than in the studio.

(417) In order to limit the potential of spoilers leaking, no scripts for season eight were printed. They were all electronic.

(418) Ramsay Bolton might be beastly to 'Reek' but in real life Alfie Allen and Iwan Rheon are good friends.

(419) Peter Dinklage is a vegetarian so the food we see Tyrion eat in the show is really a soya product or tofu.

(420) An extra from Game of Thrones said on reddit that Gethin Anthony was the friendliest and nicest cast member they met. Gethin Anthony played Renly Baratheon.

(421) Gwendoline Christie had to have her long hair cut off to play Brienne. She said this was quite difficult to do but it was obviously neccessary for the character.

(422) Pedro Pascal trained in Wushu, a Chinese martial art, to prepare for Oberyn's big fight scene with the Mountain in Game of Thrones.

(423) When we see Jon and Sansa finally have their reunion in season six they are both deliberately made to seem tentative at first because they are both in shock at seeing one another again. This builds anticipation for the hug.

(424) The fight featuring young Ned and Ser Arthur Dayne took three days to shoot.

(425) Bella Ramsey got the part of Lyanna Mormont about two weeks after the audition.

(426) Richard Madden said his Robb Stark costume had so many buckles and straps it took 40 minutes to get into it!

(427) It was reported in 2017 that Hertfordshire University hosted an 'academic conference' on Game of Thrones with guest speakers from around the world.

(428) The reason why the direwolves didn't feature so much later is that when they got bigger they had to depict them with CGI and this was expensive.

(429) Conleth Hill, who played Varys, had a memorable comic guest role in a 2017 episode of Peter Kay's Car Share.

(430) Braavos takes a lot of influence from Venice.

(431) Bella Ramsey said they really missed the Lyanna Mormont costume after ending their time on Game of Thrones.

(432) The Iron Throne is made up of swords taken from the enemies of the king who sits on it.

(433) A 2019 article in Rolling Stone ranked Joffrey Baratheon as the fourth greatest television villain of all time.

(434) The Croatian city of Dubrovnik had to implement steps to limit cruise ships in 2017 because parts of the town were becoming overwhelmed with tourists who had to come to see the place that doubled for King's Landing.

(435) Melisandre is actually a centuries-old woman who uses magic to have a youthful appearance.

(436) Bella Ramsey was very excited when a Lyanna Mormont Funko Pop was released.

(437) In the books there is more family context and historical backstory about why Alistair Thorne hates Jon Snow.

(438) Brienne's armour was designed to hide Gwendoline Christie's hips and make her look more masculine and imposing.

(439) Kit Harington was in 63 episodes as Jon Snow.

(440) They couldn't use real wolves in the show because this was not permitted under British law.

(441) When the television show was announced, Rachel Hurd-Wood was the most popular 'fancasting' choice for Sansa. Hurd-Wood played Wendy Darling in a 2003 Peter Pan film.

(442) Brian Cox said he turned down the part of Robert Baratheon because the money was not great and it wasn't a

role destined to last very long. Cox said that had he known how good the show was going to be he would have taken the part.

(443) Though he played the youngest Lannister sibling, Peter Dinklage is a few years older than Nikolaj Coster-Waldau and Lena Headey.

(444) The original concept for the title sequence was to follow the path of a raven as to flew over the places seen in the show. In the end they went for a map themed titles instead.

(445) HBO were attracted to Game of Thrones because they correctly deduced it could have world wide appeal with its medieval/fantasy aura.

(446) There are some parallels between Joffrey and Richard II. Richard II was the king of England from 1377 to 1399. He was known for his extravagant spending, disputes with his nobles, and his controversial deposition from the throne.

(447) The path to Game of Thrones becoming a television series started when David Benioff's agent sent him the Song of Ice and Fire books.

(448) Sansa has an awful time in King's Landing being tormented by Joffrey and Cersei but Sophie Turner got on great with Jack Gleeson and Lena Headey in real life and said they made her laugh a lot between takes.

(449) A season of Game of Thrones was designed to be like a ten hour film.

(450) Sophie Turner said the cast would often play Scrabble on an iPad between takes for a scene.

(451) A technology company in Britain gave their employees half of a Monday off so they could watch the simulcast of the season six Game of Thrones premiere.

(452) Bella Ramsey only found out about Lyanna Mormont's death on Game of Thrones when their mum read the script.

(453) Maisie Williams was mostly homeschooled as a youngster in Game of Thrones. A lot of child/teen actors seem to be homeschooled.

(454) In the books Brienne has a broken nose and missing teeth.

(455) The Wall stretches for hundreds of miles and is over 700 feet tall.

(456) Game of Thrones had three different shooting units in the end - each with a codename.

(457) The extras on the show said playing the Unsullied was the worst job because the costumes afforded no protection against the cold and it was also physically demanding.

(458) The prequel show House of the Dragon has been a success for HBO and most fans seem to like it. Some critics of the prequel show though feel it is quite dull and ponderous compared to Game of Thrones. House of the Dragon doesn't have much humour and takes itself very seriously. It also, unlike Game of Thrones, doesn't really give you anyone to root for. It lacks the eclectic and entertaining cast of Game of Thrones and the action, wit, and fun the base show provided. Many people seem to enjoy House of the Dragon though so it is obviously all in the eye of the beholder. You can just enjoy both shows as very different beasts.

(459) House of the Dragon was inspired by 'the Anarchy' - a period of 12th century English history. A civil war was waged between the heirs of King Henry I: his legitimate heir and daughter Matilda and his nephew and closest male heir Stephen of Blois. Rhaenyra Targaryen is based on Matilda.

(460) Extras on Game of Thrones said that playing a battlefield casualty was the best job because you could just lay down all day!

(461) The unhappy but necessary marriage between Robert and Cersei at the start of the show some parallels with the marriage of King Edward II of England and Isabella of France.

(462) Iwan Rheon tested for the part of Viserys Targaryen before he read for Jon Snow and Ramsay Snow/Bolton.

(463) Iwan Rheon also said he tested to play Daario Naharis. It feels like he tested for literally every part in the show!

(464) The fight between Brienne and the Hound was shot in the Nesjavellir area of Iceland.

(465) Jermome Flynn said the American showrunners on Game of Thrones didn't know him from anything when they cast him in the show. Being from the United States, they'd never heard of Robson & Jermome or Soldier Soldier. They just thought he was a good fit from Bronn.

(466) As an overall series, Game of Thrones has a rating of 9.2 on IMDB. This puts it in the hallowed +9 company of shows like The Sopranos, Breaking Bad and The Wire.

(467) Dracarys is High Valyrian for 'dragonfire'.

(468) Pedro Pascal taped his Game of Thrones audition on his iPhone.

(469) Carice van Houten said the worst thing about Game of Thrones for her was having to ride a horse because she is scared of horses.

(470) Isaac Hempstead Wright said that Bran's medieval wheelchair was very uncomfortable to sit in.

(471) Jonathan Pryce said that he got recognised more in public through Game of Thrones than anything else he has ever done in his long career.

(472) Over seventy actresses were tested for the part of Yara Greyjoy before Gemma Whelan was cast.

(473) The Hand of the King is the king's most senior and high ranking adviser. This is a very powerful position to hold.

(474) Gemma Whelan said she became great friends with Alfie Allen though playing Theon's sister on the show.

(475) Tom Wlaschiha played Jaqen H'ghar in Game of Thrones. Wlaschiha is a German actor and later played the character Dmitri in Stranger Things 4.

(476) Ser Jorah Mormont was nicknamed Ser Friendzone by fans because of his love for Daenerys.

(477) Nathalie Emmanuel began her career in the teen soap opera Hollyoaks.

(478) The late writer and broadcaster Clive James wrote a long essay for the New Yorker about binging Game of Thrones. His

main praise went to Charles Dance, Lena Headey, and Peter Dinklage as the Lannister characters.

(479) The Citadel is the headquarters of the order of maesters.

(480) Gemma Whelan described Game of Thrones as The Sopranos with swords.

(481) Sophie Turner's real hair colour is blonde.

(482) There is actually a YouTube video which features Tyrion slapping Joffrey for ten hours on a loop!

(483) Lena Headey said she was disappointed we never got a Cersei and Arya showdown.

(484) Gwendoline Christie was a gymnast when she was younger.

(485) George RR Martin said that 300 actresses tested for the part of Cersei.

(486) Jacob Anderson said it was quite emotional for him to take Grey Worm's armour off for the last ever time.

(487) Sophie Turner said that in the food scenes on Game of Thrones she just used to nibble a piece of bread.

(488) Nearly all of the costumes you saw in Game of Thrones were specially made in Belfast.

(489) The Unsullied costume designs originally had a spike on their helmets. This was changed though because it was too reminiscent of German soldiers in World War I.

(490) Maisie Williams said that when she started on Game of Thrones her only hope was to make enough money to buy a laptop!

(491) In the Game of Thrones scenes set up north shot in the summer they would sometimes use a filter to make it look like winter.

(492) Former cast members like Sean Bean and Jason Momoa attended the Game of Thrones season eight wrap party.

(493) Paul Kaye had to do seven auditions before he was cast as Thoros of Myr.

(494) The Iron Islands subplot involving Theon's family and the Kingsmoot is more developed in the books compared to the TV show, where it is condensed and simplified.

(495) Extras on Game of Thrones said you had a better chance of being hired as an extra if you had a beard.

(496) Richard Madden later said he wasn't paid much for his role as Robb Stark. He said he wasn't complaining though because he was young and hadn't done much and Game of Thrones put him on the map.

(497) Carice van Houten said she thinks the appeal of Game of Thrones was that it was a bit like Shakespeare in the way it held up a mirror to real events.

(498) The Iron Throne seems to have the weapon Orlando Bloom uses in Ridley Scott's Kingdom of Heaven.

(499) Daenerys was often referred to as Danny or Dany by fans of the show.

(500) David Benioff and Dan Weiss said their one regret on Game of Thrones is not bringing back Mord the Jailer - the character who imprisons Tyrion in season one. There was an abandoned plot where Mord uses the gold Tyrion gives him to open an inn and we were going to see characters use this inn from time to time.

(501) Emilia Clarke said she always adopted a straight back posture when she played Daenerys.

(502) The legendary comic book writer Alan Moore described Game of Thrones as 'The Sopranos set in Fifth-Century Dorset'. Moore said he only watched a couple of episodes.

(503) House of The Dragon star Matt Smith said he was always a big Game of Thrones fan. He said he actually met George RR Martin at a comic con before Game of Thrones had even come out on television.

(504) Emma D'Arcy, who plays Rhaenyra in House of the Dragon, said she never actually watched Game of Thrones.

(505) Emilia Clarke said her costumes on Game of Thrones were spectacular but uncomfortable to wear.

(506) Tom Wlaschiha said he would open to playing Jaqen H'ghar again in a spin-off show.

(507) Bella Ramsey said she can't bring herself to watch Pedro Pascal's death scene in Game of Thrones because they became such good friends through The Last of Us.

(508) Joseph Quinn was in a season seven Game of Thrones episode as one of the guards who won't let Arya into Winterfell. Quinn later got his breakout role as Eddie Munson

in Stranger Things 4.

(509) Bella Ramsey said that Liam Cunningham was very friendly on the set of Game of Thrones set and helped looked after her.

(510) Natalia Tena seemed to later express some disappointment that Osha was killed off in season six shortly after returning to the show. She said she would have loved to have survived.

(511) Emilia Clarke said she was too embarrassed to watch Game of Thrones with her parents because of the nudity.

(512) George RR Martin said that Winterfell is his favourite castle.

(513) The High Sparrow was sometimes compared in the media to the politicians Bernie Sanders and Jeremy Corbyn.

(514) John Bradley said he tapped into his own shyness and insecurities to play Sam Tarly.

(515) George RR Martin said it was HBO and not him who decided the television show would be called Game of Thrones rather than A Song of Ice and Fire.

(516) Jason Momoa said he really struggled to get any work when he left Game of Thrones. Fortunately though the part of Aquaman then came his way.

(517) Iwan Rheon said he was offered a lot of villain roles after Game of Thrones but tried to avoid them for fear of being typecast.

(518) Dan Weiss said he didn't let his son watch Game of Thrones until he was thirteen.

(519) In the world of Game of Thrones, having dragons is sort of like having nuclear weapons.

(520) Peter Dinklage said it is very obvious that Tyrion is in love with Daenerys.

(521) You can see a dragon theme in some of the chairs and decor at King's Landing. This indicates that the Lannisters kept some of the Targaryen furnishings in place.

(522) After shooting her last ever scene on the show, Gwendoline Christie said on Instagram - 'My heart aches with how much I will miss Ser Brienne of Tarth. But what she has inspired I will take with me. Thank you. Thank you. Thank you.'

(523) The Wall symbolises the boundary between civilisation and the unknown.

(524) Kristian Nairn said his Hodor costume was never washed so it got a bit stinky in the end.

(525) George RR Martin said that Westeros is about the size of South America.

(526) Richard Dormer said that his character Beric Dondarrion had the coolest weapon in the show - a flaming sword.

(527) Natalie Dormer, John Bradley, and House of the Dragon star Matt Smith were all in a terrible horror film called Patient Zero.

(528) The dragon necklace worn by Daenerys was commissioned by a London jewellery maker.

(529) Margaery's funnel dress in the show was based on an Alexander McQueen costume once worn by the singer Bjork.

(530) Cersei apparently had more costume changes than any other character.

(531) You can actually buy a Funko Pop Headless Ned.

(532) Jacob Anderson said he was a big fan of the show before he was cast as Grey Worm so it was very surreal to then watch it and see himself!

(533) Emilia Clarke got a tattoo of three dragons on her wrist to celebrate Game of Thrones.

(534) Lena Headey said in 2023 she is glad that Game of Thrones mania has died down.

(535) Wun Wun, who played a heroic role in the Battle of the Bastards, was the last of the giants.

(536) Jonathan Pryce said he had the easiest costume fitting of anyone on the show because the High Sparrow just wore a bit of sackcloth.

(537) Drogon is the largest of the three dragons.

(538) Maisie Williams nearly skipped her Game of Thrones audition because it clashed with a school field trip.

(539) Around 65 stuntmen worked on the episode Battle of the Bastards.

(540) The Ranker website has Tyrion Lannister voted as the most popular character in the show.

(541) House of the Dragon first season star Milly Alcock was later cast as Supergirl in the DC film universe.

(542) Ciarán Hinds said he stopped watching Game of Thrones when his character Mance Rayder died. He said he does intend to watch it all one day though.

(543) Cersei's name might have been inspired by Circe. Circe is a witch in Greek mythology.

(544) Yara Greyjoy is Asha Greyjoy in the books. They changed the name in the show because they thought Asha was too similar to Osha.

(545) Arya's sword is called Needle. It was a gift from Jon Snow.

(546) The ancestral Valyrian steel sword belonging to House Tarly is called Heartsbane. Sam steals his sword from his father and gives it to Jorah before the battle against the White Walkers.

(547) Petyr Baelish is known as Littlefinger because he was born in The Fingers (The Vale).

(548) Sophie Turner is actually allergic to horses.

(549) You can buy Game of Thrones duvets.

(550) Joffrey was often put in red as a symbol of blood and sadism.

(551) The characters of the Night's Watch don't wear hats because the producers felt it would be impossible for viewers to tell them apart. In reality though, if you were up there on the Wall in the freezing cold you'd definitely want a nice warm hat on your head.

(552) There has been a range of licenced Game of Thrones Whisky.

(553) The crypts under Winterfell and the Red Keep Dungeon are the same set.

(554) Kit Harington said that after all those years as Jon Snow he wouldn't mind playing some villains for a change.

(555) Maisie Williams said that after shooting her last ever scene for Game of Thrones she took a moment to be alone in her trailer and then went out for a 'fancy' meal.

(556) The Guardian named Battle of the Bastards as the best episode of any television show in 2016.

(557) Cersei was partly inspired by Margaret of Anjou. Margaret of Anjou (1430-1482) was the wife of King Henry VI of England and played a significant role in the Wars of the Roses. Margaret was a fierce and determined woman who fought tirelessly to protect the interests of her husband and son. As queen consort, Margaret was deeply involved in the political machinations of the court.

(558) Maisie Williams said her ambition was to be a dancer and that she fell into acting by accident.

(559) Some scientists have said that the great ice Wall in Game of Thrones would collapse under its own weight in reality.

(560) Natalie Dormer has run in the London marathon a couple of times.

(561) Kristian Nairn actually grew up within 40 miles of the location where he shot many of his scenes as Hodor.

(562) Richard Dormer, who played Beric Dondarrion, said that when he was shooting in Iceland he was so exhausted he barely took in the wonderful views.

(563) The Lannisters own gold mines but they start to dry up in the end - which doesn't help their finances.

(564) The last ever scene that Carice van Houten shot in Game of Thrones was when Melisandre lights the trench during the battle with the White Walkers.

(565) Paul Kaye said he was terrified when he first turned up to play Thoros of Myr because he had doubts about his acting. Kaye's background was in comedy.

(566) The Ironborn are known for their naval prowess and raiding skills.

(567) The origin of dragons is steeped in mythology and folklore from various cultures around the world. They are often depicted as large, serpentine creatures with wings and the ability to breathe fire. In Western mythology, dragons are often seen as malevolent creatures that hoard treasure and terrorize villages. In Eastern mythology, dragons are revered and seen as symbols of power, strength, and good fortune.

(568) The Hound has one fear - fire. This is because his brother held his head to the fire when they were children.

(569) Game of Thrones overtook The Sopranos to become the biggest ever HBO show.

(570) Jason Momoa said that when he was on Game of Thrones he stole so many props that he got warned about it!

(571) John Bradley said he is amazed he survived Game of Thrones. Each season he expected Sam to be killed off.

(572) Conleth Hill said he felt Game of Thrones was better when it was 'smaller' and had a lot of intrigue. He felt the show got a bit big and blockbuster like in its later seasons.

(573) Millie Bobby Brown, who narrowly missed out on the part of Lyanna Mormont, said she binged the whole of Game of Thrones during the pandemic lockdowns.

(574) Olivia Cooke plays the character of Alicent Hightower in House of the Dragon. Cooke said, in preparation for House of the Dragon, she binged the whole of Game of Thrones with her mother.

(575) Ryan Condal, a showrunner on House of the Dragon, said that his favourite Game of Thrones character was the Hound.

(576) Daniel Portman said that when he did his Podrick audition he pretended he'd read the books when in reality he hadn't.

(577) Winterfell is a key strategic location in the ongoing power struggles of the Seven Kingdoms.

(578) George RR Martin said the immense fame the television show gave him has been a mixed blessing.

(579) John Bradley said his most surreal moment was when he went to watch his beloved Manchester United play and David Beckham asked him for a photograph in the director's box.

(580) Ed Skrein and Michiel Huisman, the two actors who played Daario Naharis, were both in the 2023 film Rebel Moon. Ed Skrein (who was replaced by Huisman in Game of Thrones) said they got on great and became friends.

(581) In a flashback we see the young Cersei visit a witch named Maggy The Frog and hear a prophecy which says that all her children will die and a younger more beautiful woman will take away everything she has. The prophecy most likely references Daenerys but it might also explain why Cersei is so suspicious and jealous of Margery.

(582) Isaac Hempstead Wright said it was very weird going back to school after doing any shooting on Game of Thrones.

(583) George RR Martin said that King's Landing ignoring the White Walker threat can be seen as an allegory for people who ignore climate change.

(584) Carice van Houten said she was thrilled when she had a guest spot on The Simpsons.

(585) Game of Thrones was known for its shocking plot twists, making it one of the most talked-about shows of the modern era.

(586) Lena Headey said a lot of booze was drunk at the final Game of Thrones wrap party.

(587) Game of Thrones was renowned for its lavish production design, stunning visuals, and epic battle sequences. The show

felt like a big-budget movie with each episode, which contributed to its massive appeal.

(588) Emilia Clarke said she was surprised by the direction they took Daenerys in season eight.

(589) You can buy Game of Thrones collectible swords and weapons replicas.

(590) The Dorne plotline is significantly altered in the TV show, with several characters and storylines being omitted or changed.

(591) Valyrian steel and dragonglass are two materials that can kill White Walkers.

(592) Dame Diana Rigg compared Olenna Tyrell to the Borgias. The Borgias were a Spanish-Italian noble family that rose to power in the late 15th and early 16th centuries. They were known for their ruthless tactics and cunning political maneuvering.

(593) Daniel Portman said he felt the appeal of Podrick was that he was an everyman character we could relate to.

(594) Charles Dance said he found the last ever episode of Game of Thrones confusing.

(595) Alfie Allen said that occasionally someone will still come up to him on the street and complain about season eight of Game of Thrones.

(596) Kit Harington became a heart-throb as Jon Snow although in the books Jon Snow is not described as super handsome.

(597) The Rains of Castamere is a song which tells the story of the destruction of House Reyne of Castamere by House Lannister, who are renowned for their vengeful and ruthless nature. The song is a cautionary tale of the consequences of crossing the Lannisters.

(598) The famous author Salman Rushdie is a fan of Game of Thrones. He (rather snootily) described it as 'addictive garbage'.

(599) The Iron Throne symbolises power, authority, and the constant struggle for dominance.

(600) Tywin is depicted as being more of a frontline general in the show than he was in the books.

(601) Game of Thrones was often shown in bars where fans would gather to watch.

(602) Rory McCann said he thought of the Hound (once he left the employ of the Lannisters) as basically an outlaw.

(603) One of the things about Game of Thrones that made it so gripping to viewers was the sense of danger the world it depicted created. It made us feel that few of the characters were safe.

(604) James Cosmo, who played Jeor Mormont, did a Bank of Scotland commercial in 2015 in what looked a lot like his Game of Thrones costume.

(605) George RR Martin said he had the power to snub Hollywood and choose HBO to adapt his books because he didn't need the money. The question of who would pay him the most didn't come into the equation.

(606) Maisie Williams said that when a new Game of thrones episode came out she would go to her mum's house and watch it there.

(607) A historical figure who might have inspired the character of Lord Varys is Sir Francis Walsingham. Sir Francis Walsingham (c. 1532 – 1590) was an English statesman and spymaster who served as principal secretary to Queen Elizabeth I. Walsingham's spy network employed a wide range of tactics, including coded messages, intercepting letters, and using informants to gather information.

(608) The fight on the ice with the White Walkers in Beyond the Wall took five weeks to shoot.

(609) 12% of all the illegal downloading of the season six premiere through torrents occurred in Australia.

(610) Alfie Allen said that when Theon is a prisoner of Ramsay Bolton it became an interesting acting challenge for him because he had less lines and had to do a lot of acting with his eyes and face.

(611) Richard Dormer described his character Beric Dondarrion as like a slightly shambolic version of Obi-Wan Kenobi!

(612) Emilia Clarke and Kit Harington never did any scenes together until season seven.

(613) There was a $20 million marketing campaign to promote season eight.

(614) Some fans of the books were disappointed that Ser Barristan Selmy was killed by the Sons of the Harpy in season

five because the book version of the character definitely wouldn't have been killed like that.

(615) In a retrospective when the show ended, The Guardian newspaper ranked Blackwater as the greatest Game of Thrones episode.

(616) Gemma Whelan said she was disappointed by the backlash against season eight because she thought it was a good ending.

(617) Hafthor Bjornsson, who played the Mountain in Game of Thrones, broke the world deadlift record in 2020.

(618) Alfie Allen said he was once on holiday in Thailand and a man tried to sell him some Game of Thrones DVDs (which had obviously fallen off the back of a lorry) on a beach. The man then did a double take when he realised that Alfie was Theon Greyjoy in the show!

(619) Iwan Rheon described Ramsay Bolton as a mixture of the Joker and Dennis the Menace. Dennis the Menace is a character in the Beano comics. He's a badly behaved kid always up to mischief.

(620) Joffrey considers calling his Valyrian steel sword Stormbringer and Terminus. Stormbringer is the name of a sword in Michael Moorcock's Elric series.

(621) Shortly after they filmed the Dothraki wedding early in the show, there was a storm in Malta which destroyed a number of props.

(622) Margaery's (purple) wedding dress for her marriage to Joffrey was the most expensive costume to make in the show.

It featured silver-plated cord and thorns made of Czech glass.

(623) You can buy Game of Thrones pillow cases.

(624) When the first two episodes of Game of Thrones were available for review a number of newspaper critics were very sniffy and cast doubt on the show's prospects. Nancy deWolf in The Wall Street Journal called it a 'adolescent-boy-action-show' while The Washington Post called the show a 'slog' to get through.

(625) There is a Game of Thrones board game. The second edition blurb went like this -

'King Robert Baratheon is dead, and the lands of Westeros brace for battle. In the second edition of A Game of Thrones: The Board Game, three to six players take on the roles of the great Houses of the Seven Kingdoms of Westeros, as they vie for control of the Iron Throne through the use of diplomacy and warfare. Based on the best-selling A Song of Ice and Fire series of fantasy novels by George R.R. Martin, A Game of Thrones is an epic board game in which it will take more than military might to win. Will you take power through force, use honeyed words to coerce your way onto the throne, or rally the townsfolk to your side? Through strategic planning, masterful diplomacy, and clever card play, spread your influence over Westeros!'

(626) When they were casting the kids in Game of Thrones, HBO did some casting calls at schools in England. This is how Sophie Turner got the part of Sansa.

(627) The summer palace of Malta's president was used for MagistarIllyrio's manse across the Narrow Sea.

(628) House Tyrell's motto is "Growing Strong".

(629) The Dreadfort is the seat of House Bolton.

(630) Robb Stark's role in the show was expanded somewhat because the showrunners liked the performance of Richard Madden.

(631) Jacob Anderson said Grey Worm's costume was so uncomfortable it left him with scars.

(632) George RR Martin stopped writing for the television show after the fourth season because he wanted to focus on the books.

(633) Robert Baratheon was partly inspired by Edward IV.

(634) It has been said that literally every young male actor in Britain auditioned for Jon Snow.

(635) Jason Momoa was another cast member on Game of Thrones who said he was scared of horses.

(636) Lena Headey said she didn't watch House of the Dragon because it would be too 'weird'.

(637) Iain Glen said he was pretty lucky on Game of Thrones because a lot of his stuff was shot in the warm locations.

(638) Gemma Whelan named Battle of the Bastards as her favourite episode.

(639) Charles Dance was apparently George RR Martin's first choice for the part of Tywin.

(640) The dagger that Bronn always has fastened behind him looks a lot like the Kukri blade used by Gurkha soldiers.

(641) When Tyrion slaps Joffrey in season two after they are attacked by the starving crowd, they do a clever trick by having Joffrey sitting down so that he's the same height as Tyrion. The scene is symbolic of Joffrey's lack of authority over Tyrion.

(642) Cotton wool was sometimes used for falling snow in the show.

(643) The Winds of Winter is unusual for the use of piano in the score. It works amazingly well though.

(644) The direwolves in the show were often depicted on set by a tennis ball on a stick and then put in later with special effects.

(645) Jonathan Pryce said he didn't think of the High Sparrow as a villian.

(646) Hannah Murray had never seen Game of Thrones when she got her Gilly audition because she was in student accommodation and didn't even have a television.

(647) Ravens are the carrier pigeons of the Game of Thrones world and used to send long distance messages.

(648) Gemma Whelan said that Tyrion was her favourite character.

(649) Members of the Night's Watch are called Crows by the Free Folk/Wildings.

(650) To prepare for her Game of Thrones audition, Gemma Whelan binged ten episodes of the show over two nights.

(651) Isaac Hempstead Wright combined playing Bran with going to school. He thinks this helped him to have a more normal childhood than some child actors.

(652) Kit Harington and John Bradley became good friends offscreen too - mirroring the Jon/Sam friendship in Game of Thrones.

(653) According to the Hollywood reporter, the main cast members were on one million dollars an episode in the last season.

(654) Kit Harington said that when he appears in a play he doesn't mind if some people only came because he was Jon Snow in Game of Thrones.

(655) George RR Martin said he didn't like the hunting scene leading to King Robert's death because there were so few extras and characters as part of the hunt.

(656) One of the scenes Kit Harington had to do for his audition was Jon Snow's first meeting with Tyrion.

(657) Thomas Brodie Sangster, who played Jojen Reed, said he wasn't very familiar with Game of Thrones when he was offered an audition. He said he only realised how big the show was when his friends told him.

(658) The producers would sometimes write a fake death scene purely to prank a member of the cast!

(659) The pyromancer Hallyne is played by Roy Dotrice. Roy

Dotrice had narrated the audiobooks of George RR Martin's novels. Roy was supposed to play Grandmaester Pycelle but ill health prevented him from taking this slightly larger role.

(660) You can, should you wish, buy Game of Thrones themed soap.

(661) George RR Martin said that if he does ever finish his book series the books will be 'quite different' from what happened at the end of Game of Thrones.

(662) Shooting scenes in Iceland in the winter months was very difficult because the days are much shorter and daylight is at a premium. The twilight though was extraordinary.

(663) The Iron Bank may have been inspired by the Medici family. The Medici family, also known as the House of Medici, was a powerful and influential Italian banking family that rose to prominence in the 15th century. Originally from Florence, the Medici family played a significant role in the development of the city as a major cultural and economic center during the Renaissance.

(664) Aiden Gillan said he tried to make Baelish witty and non-threatening so that the character's manipulations would be more believable.

(665) Iwan Rheon got his start in acting on the Welsh language soap opera Pobol y Cwm.

(666) Hodor actor Kiristian Nairn said he never met Charles Dance when he was on the show but did meet him in real life for the first time a few years ago.

(667) Bernard Cornwell, who wrote the books The Last

Kingdom television show was based on, called Game of Thrones 'dull' in a 2015 interview. Cornwell said Game of Thrones was filled with gratuitous nudity to keep viewers interested.

(668) George RR Martin said that Fritz Leiber was an influence on his work. Fritz Leiber (1910-1992) was an American writer known for his work in science fiction, fantasy, and horror. He is best known for his Fafhrd and the Gray Mouser series, which follows the adventures of two sword-and-sorcery heroes in the fictional world of Nehwon.

(669) One of the brilliant things about the episode Blackwater is that the viewer is conflicted about the outcome of the battle. We like the idea of Stannis winning and deposing the awful Joffrey but at the same time we can't help but root for Tyrion and Bronn - who are defending the city against Stannis.

(670) George RR Martin's books have been described as 'dirty medievalism'. That is to say a fantasy story but one grounded in a medieval realism.

(671) The Unsullied army was often really 70 extras in front of a green screen. Digital effects would then be used to make the army look much bigger.

(672) Sophie Turner said that Jack Gleeson would often perform comedy raps while he was waiting to do his Joffrey scenes.

(673) The extras on Game of Thrones were given hot chocolate to drink on cold days.

(674) Jamie Lannister was considered to be a legendary fighter

before he lost his hand.

(675) The Red Keep is the name of the castle in King's Landing. The castle is a symbol of power.

(676) In the television show, Jamie enlists Bronn as his right-hand man in later seasons. This partnership does not happen in the books.

(677) Joe Dempsie said that besides Jon Snow he auditioned for two other roles before being cast as Gendry.

(678) Jerome Flynn said British fans of the books were dismayed when he was cast as Bronn because they mainly knew him from his cheesy Robson & Jerome singing days!

(679) HBO first ordered Game of Thrones way back in 2008.

(680) Lyanna Mormont demonstrates that leadership and courage are not constricted by age or gender.

(681) A common online question, believe it or not, is whether or not Bella Ramsey is related to the bad tempered television chef Gordon Ramsay. The answer is of course NO. Their surnames aren't even spelled the same way!

(682) Minnie Driver, who was a Game of Thrones superfan, joked that she begged the producers for a part in the show.

(683) Maisie Williams was originally in the mix to play Ellie in the HBO screen adaptation of The Last of Us. This part was eventually played by Maisie's Game of Thrones co-star Bella Ramsey. Maisie is several years older than Bella Ramsey and had aged out of contention by the time the show was ready to begin production.

(684) Much of the cast had to do fight and stunt training for Game of Thrones.

(685) Game of Thrones was praised for its strong female characters.

(686) Game of Thrones and George RR Martin took a degree of inspiration from the Lord of the Rings books.

(687) For a time after its release, Battle of the Bastards had a perfect 10 out of 10 score on IMDB.

(688) Bella Ramsey's Last of Us co-star Pedro Pascal was obviously in Game of Thrones too but he was killed off before Bella joined the show. Pedro and Bella only met for the first time when they started shooting The Last of Us.

(689) Peter Dinklage has played Tyrion for a Saturday Night Live spoof on television.

(690) Preview 'screeners' of season six for critics were cancelled to avoid any risk of spoilers.

(691) Kit Harington said that when he first got the Game of Thrones scripts he thought it would be impossible to translate them into a television show.

(692) Sophie Turner said the food used for Sansa's wedding to Tyrion was awful so you just had to push it around the plate and pretend you were eating.

(693) After shooting Ned Stark's death, Sean Bean then had to film further scenes in Malta. This is obviously because scenes and episodes were not shot in order.

(694) Emilia Clarke said in an interview that she wouldn't be watching House of the Dragon. Emilia said watching the show would be like 'going to someone else's school reunion'.

(695) It often took an entire year to film a season of Game of Thrones.

(696) Sophie Turner said she never read the books while she was in the show.

(697) Kit Harington later said he was glad the original pilot got canned because he didn't think he was very good in it.

(698) The candles in Game of Thrones were lit by a blowtorch on the set to save time.

(699) Sophie Turner said that when she started on Game of Thrones she wasn't treated like a celebrity at school because none of her friends there were even old enough to watch the show.

(700) Bella Ramsey said they STILL haven't watched the whole of Game of Thrones but might do so one day.

(701) On average, Game of thrones cost about $100 million a season to make.

(702) When she was cast as Yara Greyjoy, Gemma Whelan got told off by the producers for revealing this online. The protocol is that shows announce the casting in their own time.

(703) The Dornish scenes in Game of Thrones were shot in Seville.

(704) The Hound eats some raw pig feet when he's on the road with Arya. Yuck!

(705) A poll for Entertainment Weekly ranked Cersei Lannister as the best villain in the show.

(706) Peter Dinklage said he was hesitant about doing Game of Thrones at first because he assumed it was some silly fantasy show where they'd put him in pointy shoes and a large hat.

(707) George RR Martin said he disagreed with the television show's decision not to bring back Catelyn Stark as Lady Stoneheart.

(708) Joe Dempsie said it was a bit weird shooting the love scene between Arya and Gendry in season eight because he had known Maisie Williams since she was eleven years-old.

(709) Nikolaj Coster-Waldau said some of his actor friends in Denmark laughed when he told them he was going to be in a new HBO show about dragons.

(710) In 2018, characters from Game of Thrones appeared on postage stamps in Britain.

(711) The villain Vecna in Stranger Things 4 was inspired by the Night King in Game of Thrones.

(712) In the books, the Night's watch have a raven which can speak (like a parrot) and seems to understand what is being said by people. They dropped this in the television show because they thought it was a trifle silly.

(713) Karen Gillan said she auditioned for Game of Thrones before she landed the part of Amy Pond in Doctor Who. It is

sometimes presumed Gillan tested to play Sansa but she is eight years older than Sophie Turner so this might possibly have been another part.

(714) The prostitute Ros is a character invented for the television show. Ros is a composite of characters from the books.

(715) Peter Dinklage was in 68 episodes in all.

(716) In the first episode/second pilot we hear Arya mention that Jamie is the Queen's brother. This line was was pointedly added because in the scrapped pilot this fact wasn't made clear and the audience needed this information to understand that Jamie and Cersei are in an incestuous relationship.

(717) The Wall is 1,000 leagues from King's Landing. It takes an hour to walk a single league.

(718) The fate of the legendary swordsman Syrio Forel is left somewhat ambiguous after he saves Arya in The Pointy End. We can probably presume that he sacrificed himself though because he only had a wooden training sword and was never seen again.

(719) One of the few scenes from the scrapped pilot which made it into the first episode was the conversation between Ned and Robert in the crypt.

(720) Jerome Flynn as Bronn makes his first appearance in Cripples, Bastards, and Broken Things.

(721) Games of Thrones is occasionally cited as a show that wasn't diverse enough in its casting. In response to this, casting director Nina Gold said they simply cast characters

based on what they were described as looking like in the books. She also pointed out that they did have prominent black characters like Grey Worm and Missandei.

(722) Cersei Lannister is known for her cunning and ruthless nature, embodying the phrase, "A lion does not concern itself with the opinions of sheep."

(723) NFL legend Aaron Rodgers made a blink and you'll miss it cameo in the season eight episode The Bells.

(724) The title sequence of the show changes to reflect the locations that will be featured.

(725) Game of Thrones was broadcast in over 207 countries and territories worldwide.

(726) Game of Thrones did some location shooting in Morocco.

(727) The phrase "Valar Morghulis" translates to "All men must die".

(728) Bella Ramsey appeared in nine episodes of Game of Thrones.

(729) Sean Bean kicked Ned Stark's prop head around in a game of football after his death scene.

(730) There were 42 weeks of post-production after series eight completed filming.

(731) Jaime Lannister is a horrible man at the start of Game of Thrones but he does have an arc of redemption where he becomes a better person. Jamie later travels to Winterfell to

help fight the White Walkers.

(732) Game of Thrones was so popular that people named their pets after characters in the show.

(733) Jojen Reed is a greenseer, with the ability to see into the past and future through his dreams. He travels with Bran Stark and his sister Meera to help him on his journey beyond the Wall.

(734) Rose Leslie said her siblings were big Game of Thrones fans and were actually more excited than her when she landed the part of Ygritte.

(735) There was a 2012 Game of Thrones action role-playing video game. Developed by Cyanide and published by Atlus USA, the game follows two original characters, Mors Westford and Alester Sarwyck, who are sent on a quest that takes them across the Seven Kingdoms of Westeros. James Cosmo and Conleth Hill reprised their roles from the television series as Jeor Mormont and Varys. The game got mixed reviews from critics.

(736) The RR in George RR Martin's name stands for Raymond Richard.

(737) David Benioff & Dan Weiss directed the last ever episode of Game of Thrones. They probably regret that now!

(738) Game of Thrones holds the record for the most Emmy Awards won by a scripted drama television series.

(739) Podrick Payne had a very minimal role in the show early on but then got more scenes later.

(740) Before the Battle of the Blackwater, King Joffrey is very boastful and takes great delight in brandishing his new sword. He declares that Stannis would be a fool to come near him. Of course, this is a hollow boast full of meaningless bluster. Joffrey wouldn't last five seconds in a fight with Stannis!

(741) Waymar Royce was originally played by Jamie Campbell Bower but the scene was reshot with Rob Ostlere. Jamie Campbell Bower later played the villain Vecna/Henry Creel in Stranger Things 4.

(742) Games of Thrones pulls a memorable twist in season one with the death of Ned Stark. Sean Bean has top billing in the credits and is the lead character in the show.

(743) Bella Ramsey had to do school homework in the Lyanna Mormont costume during breaks on Game of Thrones.

(744) Richard Madden said he rather enjoyed just being a viewer and not knowing what was going to happen in the show after he left Game of Thrones.

(745) Bella Ramsey said it wasn't too difficult to maintain the stoic and stern persona of Lyanna Mormont on Game of Thrones.

(746) Benjen Stark is the younger brother of Eddard Stark, and a member of the Night's Watch. Benjen goes missing early in the series and his fate remains a mystery for much of the story.

(747) IKEA rugs were used to construct the fur coats the men of the Night's Watch wear.

(748) Sansa's direwolf was named Lady. In real life, Sophie

Turner adopted the Mahlek Northern Inuit pup who played Lady.

(749) Dean-Charles Chapman, who played Tommen Barathon, said that Isaac Hempstead Wright, who played Bran, was his best friend on the show.

(750) When they were shooting Game of Thrones in Spain one time, some photographers managed to get up on a hill and take secret pictures of the scenes being shot. This sort of stuff is a nightmare for a television or film production.

(751) They had the legendary swordsman Ser Arthur Dayne use two swords in the show as a means to make him feel almost like a superhero. Wielding two swords in a fight would obviously be impossible for mere mortals.

(752) Pedro Pascal said he did read some of the books to prepare for playing Oberyn.

(753) Samwell Tarly is based on Samwise Gamgee from The Lord of the Rings.

(754) At its height, Game of Thrones required 151 sets for its production.

(755) Bella Ramsey said they would always talk to the extras on Game of Thrones because sometimes extras can be a bit forgotten on a big film set.

(756) Jamie Bamber auditioned for the part of Jamie Lannister. Bamber is best known for his role as Lee Adama in Battlestar Galactica.

(757) Maisie Williams is right-handed but had to learn to use a

weapon with her other hand because Arya Stark is left-handed.

(758) David Benioff & Dan Weiss said that rather than bother with critics reviews they would often look at the IMDB rating of a new Game of Thrones episode to get a guage on whether it had gone down well or not.

(759) Peter Dinklage said that after shooting scenes in hot weather in Croatia he would often go and jump in the sea to cool off

(760) An extra on Game of Thrones would usually get paid about £100 a day.

(761) Peter Dinklage said there was a lot of 'corpsing' on Game of Thrones and actors flubbing takes by laughing. He said that Lena Headey and Jerome Flynn would always make him laugh during scenes.

(762) Sam Coleman, who played the young Hodor, said he felt a bit out of place at the auditions because all the other kids going up for (young) Hodor were younger than him. Happily though he got the part in the end.

(763) The producers said the worst thing about shooting in Northern Ireland was that it got dark really early in the winter.

(764) John Bradley named Battle of the Bastards as his favourite Game of Thrones episode.

(765) Emilia Clarke said one of the hazards of doing so much outdoor shooting was bird poop!

(766) Maisie Williams said it only dawned on her how big Game of Thrones was when she got mobbed at the season three premiere.

(767) Dan Weiss and David Benioff said the Red Wedding was the incident in the books that made them decide they HAD to turn George RR Martin's books into a television show.

(768) Maisie Williams said it was freezing in Northern Ireland but the nice people there made it a pleasure to shoot in.

(769) Rory McCann had to spend about two hours in the makeup chair to be turned into the Hound.

(770) The stairs where Gregor and Sandor fight in season eight was a set specially built for this scene.

(771) There were a number of leaks for season seven because HBO were hacked. There were some arrests in India as a consequence.

(772) Liam Cunningham said he never read a single page of any of the books Game of Thrones was based on.

(773) Bella Ramsey said they had no idea that acting might actually be a realistic career until Game of Thrones.

(774) The Prince and Princess of Wales (William & Kate) were famously big fans of Game of Thrones.

(775) After being cast in Games of Thrones, Bella Ramsey would sometimes pretend to be Lyanna Mormont at the family dinner table. Bella's family found this a bit annoying!

(776) The seventh season of Game of Thrones was illegally

downloaded more than a billion times according to piracy tracking firm Muso.

(777) Stephen Dillane, who played Stannis, later said that he genuinely had no idea what was happening in most of his scenes or what his character was supposed to be. Stephen's complaint was that the direction was vague. Despite this though his performance was brilliant.

(778) Dan Weiss and David Benioff said they found it impossible to cast Khalo Drogo but eventually found a fancasting website which suggested Jason Momoa. So they took the advice of the fan website and cast him!

(779) Kit Harington knew Gemma Whelan before Game of Thrones because they were in a yoga class together.

(780) Khaleesi is a term for Queen in Dothraki.

(781) Conleth Hill said he was disappointed that Varys didn't have scenes with Littlefinger later in the show because these two characters were built up as scheming rivals early on.

(782) George RR Martin said he rejected film offers for his Song of Ice and Fire books because he felt it would only work as a long form television show.

(783) Nikolaj Coster-Waldau said that after they finished shooting the Game of Thrones pilot he never expected the show to be picked up or become a success.

(784) The Iron Throne in the books is made up of a 1000 swords. In the show they had a lot less.

(785) In 2023 it was calculated that there are about 70 million

google searches a year for Game of Thrones.

(786) Hannah Murray, who played Gilly, and Joe Dempsie, who played Gendry, were both in a British show called Skins when they were younger. They said they were a bit disappointed their characters in Game of Thrones didn't interact.

(787) Jerome Flynn hadn't acted for ten years when he got the part of Bronn. He had decided to take a hiatus from acting until an interesting part came along. Jerome said another factor in taking the Game of Thrones job was that he had run out of money!

(788) The Dorne plot in the show was added late and suffered from production trouble and a lack of time.

(789) When they filmed The Long Night episode, the frozen actors would race for the space heaters to warm up between takes.

(790) Maisie Williams blamed the modern coffee cup container being left in a season eight scene on the cast and crew being exhausted after filming at night for weeks on end.

(791) Ramsay Bolton's weapon of choice is the bow and arrow. This is one reason (besides the fact he has a bigger army) why he refuses to have a one on one fight with Jon Snow. Ramsay is well aware that Jon Snow is probably a much better swordsman than him.

(792) Pilou Asbæk and Patrick Malahide played the Greyjoy brothers in Game of Thrones but in real life Malahide is 37 years older than Asbæk.

(793) It is implied that Davos has a wife and other sons but

this is forgotten later on.

(794) In the episode The Winds of Winter, Qyburn bribes the King's Landing street urchins with candied plums. Sugared fruits were eaten by aristocrats in olden times.

(795) George RR Martin said that HBO didn't want to have Rickon Stark in the show but he persuaded them to include the character. Rickon's only function in Game of Thrones seems to be as a way for Ramsay to anger Jon Snow before the Battle of the Bastards.

(796) Kristian Nairn said that Hodor's sacrifice in The Door was voluntary because Hodor saw protecting Bran as his most important duty in life.

(797) Robin Arryn is a weasely looking child in most of the show but when he makes an appearance in the last ever episode he has become a surprisingly handsome and dashing young man.

(798) Myranda, the kennelmaster's daughter and Ramsay's lover, is a character invented for the television show.

(799) Emilia Clarke denied that she was responsible for the coffee container left in a season eight scene. Emilia said that as an English person she only drank tea!

(800) Nikolaj Coster-Waldau broke a rib shooting a scene for season three.

(801) Sophie Turner sometimes wore a wig as Sansa in the show.

(802) It was director Neil Marshall who suggested Stanis

playing a hands-on role in the Battle of Blackwater.

(803) The Wilding giants were depicted on the set by a pole with a ball where the giant's eyeline was supposed to be. The giants were then added in during post-production with special effects.

(804) The battle of the Blackwater takes place during the day in the books. The battle takes place at night in the television show. The reason they did this was because a battle during the day would have required many more extras and special effects to pull off.

(805) Alfie Allen also auditioned for the part of Jon Snow before being cast as Theon.

(806) Blackwater takes place entirely at King's Landing. It was a first for the show to have an episode take place in one location.

(807) Carice Van Houten was asked to audition for the part of Cersei Lannister but couldn't do the audition in the end because she was too busy. When she became available again she was cast as Melisandre.

(808) In the emotional scene in episode one of season eight where Sam learns that Daenerys executed his father and brother, John Bradley did the scene in one take.

(809) In the books, the Moon Door at the Eyrie was a side door rather than an opening on the floor.

(810) A full sized dragon is 230 feet long.

(811) Jason Momoa performed a haka at his audition. A haka is

Maori war dance. The New Zealand rugby union team famously do a haka before their games as a sort of formal challenge to their opponents.

(812) We see Tommen's pet cat Ser Pounce in the episode Oathkeeper. The cat used in the show constantly refused to jump on the bed and was badly behaved - which probably explains why the cat didn't return to Game of Thrones.

(813) For the dragon riding scenes, Emilia Clarke and Kit Harington had to sit atop a giant mechanical bull type machine which would jolt them around.

(814) Tywin Lannister is not a big fan of mutton. He gives his mutton supper to Arya.

(815) Neil Marshall, who cut his teeth making horror films, came up with the more gruesome flourishes in Blackwater.

(816) At his wedding festivities, Joffrey cuts open a pigeon pie from which live pigeons fly out. They actually used to do this at medieval banquet celebrations.

(817) Peter Dinklage used to be in a punk band in the 1990s.

(818) George RR Martin wrote The Lion and the Rose and had wanted the entire episode to to be set at King's Landing and revolve around the wedding. He wasn't allowed to do this though because there were other plot threads the producers needed to keep moving.

(819) Derek Halligan was originally cast as Alliser Thorne but he was replaced by Owen Teale before shooting began.

(820) In the books, Roose Bolton had a 'non bastard' son

named Domeric who died. This character was not mentioned in the television show.

(821) A lot of people think they spied Gandalf's sword from Lord of the Rings embedded in the Iron Throne.

(822) Bella Ramsey said that, through friends, they have watched the clip of Lyanna Mormont dying in Game of Thrones many times!

(823) Kit Harington wore heeled shoes as Jon Snow to make him seem taller.

(824) The sigil of House Greyjoy is a Kraken against a black background.

(825) The correct way to say Khaleesi is actually KHAH-lay-see. Jorah was getting it wrong!

(826) The sigil of House Arryn is a bird on a blue background.

(827) The director Neil Marshall was not very familiar with Game of Thrones when he was hired to direct Blackwater and had to binge season one to get up to speed.

(828) House Lannister's sigil is a golden lion with a crimson background.

(829) David Benioff said he hasn't watched Game of Thrones since it ended. Dan Weiss on the other hand said he did a rewatch with his family.

(830) There is an attraction between Grey Worm and Missandei in the show. This doesn't happen in the books because Missandei is about ten years old.

(831) After the end of Game of Thrones, Dan Weiss and David Benioff were offered a lucrative contract where they would have a producer credit on all prequels and spin-offs. They turned this down though because they were not comfortable with the idea of getting paid for a show they had little to do with.

(832) The ale drunk in the show is really just coloured water.

(833) Dan Weiss and David Benioff both said their favourite character was Hodor.

(834) Dorne is patently inspired by Spain.

(835) The cast were given hot water bottles on Game of Thrones when shooting scenes during chilly weather.

(836) Pedro Pascal, who played Oberyn Martell, was a big fan of the show and lobbied to get a part.

(837) Carice Van Houten said she wasn't told much about her character Melisandre and thinks this was beneficial because it gave her more freedom to craft her own performance.

(838) Game of Thrones had the biggest cast on television with over 200 speaking roles.

(839) Alfie Allen as Theon has more lines in season two than anyone except Peter Dinklage as Tyrion.

(840) The crew was allowed to film on glaciers and protected areas of Iceland.

(841) The director Neil Marshall said the nudity in Blackwater was nothing to do with him and inserted on the insistence of a

producer.

(842) At the start of season four we see King Joffrey claim credit for defeating Stannis on the Blackwater - despite the fact that Joffrey played no part in the battle and refused to fight.

(843) Season two cost $70 million to produce.

(844) In the tavern scene in Two Swords, Rory McCann did so many takes of the Hound drinking Polliver's ale that he felt sick in the end.

(845) In all, four different fields were used to shoot the battle in Battle of the Bastards.

(846) Sean Bean and Peter Dinklage did not have to audition for Game of Thrones. They were simply offered their respective parts and accepted.

(847) Some of the details of the battle in Battle of the Bastards were changed during filming due to budget restrictions. It all worked out fine in the end though.

(848) The casting people on Game of Thrones said they didn't cast Millie Bobby Brown as Lyanna Mormont because, despite being about the same age as Bella Ramsay, she just looked a little bit too young for the character. Brown's audition was apparently very good though.

(849) Battle of the Bastards was time consuming to shoot because the weather kept changing during the battle sequence shoot - which is a nightmare for continuity.

(850) It is often reported that Jerome Flynn and Lena Headey

were kept apart on Game of Thrones because the pair (who were once in a relationship together) didn't get on. Jerome Flynn said this story is nonsense and that he gets on fine with Lena. He pointed out that Cersei and Bronn were (briefly) in a scene together in season three. That said though, it is rather odd that we never see Bronn and Cersei have a single conversation in the show.

(851) The second episode of season eight was uploaded early by mistake.

(852) Kit Harington was one of the last actors to be cast on the show.

(853) The Great Sept of Baelor is a massive religious structure in the city of King's Landing and the primary place of worship for the Faith of the Seven, the dominant religion in Westeros. The Sept is ultimately destroyed in a devastating act of terrorism orchestrated by Cersei.

(854) Alliser Thorne is the master-at-arms of the Night's Watch and a seasoned warrior with a gruff manner. Thorne is known for his harsh training methods and strict discipline, often clashing with Jon Snow.

(855) Jared Harris auditioned to play the High Sparrow. Harris was a big Game of Thrones fan.

(856) The Long Night is the longest episode at 81 minutes.

(857) Dean-Charles Chapman said that the first scenes he had as Tommen Baratheon was when Joffrey died. He said what he remembered most about that was how the cast members were upset to be saying goodbye to Jack Gleeson.

(858) Game of Thrones is credited with pumping hundreds of millions of pounds into the economy of Northern Ireland.

(859) Outlander star Sam Heughan said he auditioned more than once for Game of Thrones but - alas - didn't get cast. He is believed to have auditioned for the parts of Renly and Loras.

(860) Sibel Kekilli said she was unhappy that her character Shae testified against Tyrion at his (sham) trial as she felt this was out of character.

(861) Davos Seaworth has seven sons in the books but there is only one seen in the show.

(862) The Massacre of Glencoe is another real historical event which may have influenced the Red Wedding. The Massacre of Glencoe, also known as the Glencoe Massacre, took place in the early hours of 13 February 1692 in the Glen Coe valley in the Scottish Highlands. The massacre was carried out by members of the Campbell clan. A detachment of Campbell soldiers, led by Captain Robert Campbell of Glenlyon, were sent to Glencoe under the guise of seeking shelter. The MacDonalds, bound by the laws of hospitality, welcomed the soldiers into their homes. However, in the early hours of the morning, the soldiers turned on their hosts and carried out a brutal massacre, killing 38 men, women, and children.

(863) Dame Diana Rigg was a big sex symbol in the 1960s for her iconic role as Emma Peel in the cult action/spy show The Avengers.

(864) Liam Cunningham took home a Dothraki sword as a momento when the show ended.

(865) The battle in Battle of the Bastards was shot at Saintfield. Saintfield is a privately owned field near Belfast.

(866) Emilia Clarke said she had to do about 28 takes of Daenerys eating the horse heart.

(867) Maisie Williams and Sophie Turner have matching tattoos. The tattoo marks the date they learned they had been cast in Game of Thrones.

(868) Emilia Clarke used to work in a call centre before she became a famous actor.

(869) The late Queen Elizabeth II visited the Game of Thrones set and viewed the Iron Throne.

(870) Because Bella Ramsey was only a little kid on Game of Thrones, the rest of the cast were very parental and protective.

(871) Jonathan Pryce said he turned down a role in Game of Thrones in season one and only took the part of the High Sparrow later because the money was too good to turn down.

(872) Some of the wigs worn by main cast members in the show cost $7,000.

(873) George RR Martin said his wife made him promise that Arya Stark would make it to the final book.

(874) Although most of it was discarded for not being good enough, a few scenes from the pilot did still make it into the first episode along with the reshoots.

(875) 52,000 bags of paper snow were used over the course of

Game of Thrones.

(876) Ser Jorah Mormont is described as overweight and not very attractive in the books. Iain Glen's version of the character was more dashing than the literary version.

(877) Jack Gleeson retired from acting after his role as Joffrey finished in Game of Thrones. However, he obviously changed his mind about that because is acting again now.

(878) Natalia Tena, who played Osha, played Nymphadora Tonks in the Harry Potter franchise.

(879) Casterly Rock was inspired by the Rock of Gibraltar. Gibraltar is a British Overseas Territory located on the southern tip of the Iberian Peninsula, bordered by Spain. It is known for its iconic Rock of Gibraltar, a limestone promontory that rises 1,398 feet above sea level and offers stunning views of the surrounding area. Gibraltar is a strategic location due to its position at the entrance to the Mediterranean Sea and has a long history of military fortifications and battles.

(880) The conclusion to the trial by combat battle in The Mountain and the Viper was originally going to be even more gruesome. It's hard to imagine how much more gruesome it could have been!

(881) The cast were not told much about the dwarf comedy scene during the Purple wedding episode so that their reactions would be genuinely bemused and horrified. This presumably didn't apply to Jack Gleeson as Joffrey arranged it.

(882) Charles Dance did not have to audition for his part in the show. Even before the show started he was a fan favourite

suggestion to play Tywin.

(883) George RR Martin said the book version of Littlefinger would never have handed Sansa over to Ramsay Bolton.

(884) Bella Ramsey went from Game of Thrones to playing Mildred Hubble in the kids show The Worst Witch. You could describe that as an interesting change of pace!

(885) Game of Thrones features a wide range of architectural styles, from the towering castles of the noble houses to the rustic villages of the common folk.

(886) Julian Glover, who played Grand Maester Pycelle, has been acting since the early 1960s. Julian has been in big films like Indiana Jones and the Last Crusade, The Empire Strikes Back, and For Your Eyes Only.

(887) Game of Thrones was the first professional acting job for Maisie Williams.

(888) The Faith of the Seven is the predominant religion in the Seven Kingdoms of Westeros. It is a polytheistic religion that worships seven gods, each representing a different aspect of life. These gods are the Father, the Mother, the Warrior, the Maiden, the Smith, the Crone, and the Stranger.

(889) Game of Thrones was the first television role for Kit Harington.

(890) Around 1,300 medieval shields were built to use in the show.

(891) Game of Thrones is the most watched HBO show of all time.

(892) According to a poll, 21% of American viewers said they were angry about how season eight turned out.

(893) Many of the shooting locations in Game of thrones have benefited from a boost in tourism by fans of the show.

(894) The show's iconic catchphrase, "Winter is coming," has become a popular meme and cultural reference.

(896) Daenerys was supposed to have purple eyes like the books but Emilia Clarke found the contacts too difficult to act with.

(897) Mark Strong is often alleged to have been offered the part of Stannis Baratheon. Strong is said to have turned the part down because he had just been cast in another show and wasn't available.

(898) The show's production team faced severe challenges filming in adverse weather conditions.

(899) Emilia Clarke said she found the nude scenes she had to do in the show difficult.

(900) Tormund Giantsbane clearly has a crush on Brienne but sadly for him Brienne is not interested. Brienne is in love with Jamie Lannister.

(901) Joe Dempsie, who played Gendry, was openly critical of the character development of the show in season seven.

(902) Jeyne Westerling was Robb Stark's love interest in the books. They obviously replaced this character in the show.

(903) The iconic Iron Throne in the show was made of

fiberglass covered in a metallic paint to give it a realistic look.

(904) Beric Dondarrion is the leader of the Brotherhood Without Banners, a group of outlaws who fight for justice and protection of the common people in the Riverlands. Beric is most well-known for being repeatedly resurrected by the red priest Thoros of Myr, using the power of the Lord of Light. Each time he is resurrected, Beric loses a piece of himself and becomes less and less like the man he used to be. Despite his tragic fate, Beric remains a noble character who fights for justice and the innocent, even at great personal cost.

(905) Charles Dance said he didn't think of Tywin Lannister as a villain but merely a man of principles - however skewed those principles might be.

(906) The cast had to endure sub-zero temperatures and snowstorms in some of the Iceland location shoots.

(907) Jack Gleeson is obviously nothing like the sadistic Joffrey in real life. Jack is a very funny and friendly chap offscreen so it was obviously a good piece of acting!

(908) Iwan Rheon said that it wasn't too much of an ordeal playing an evil character like Ramsay Bolton. Iwan said what helped is that Ramsay, despite the awful things he does, is actually quite a cheerful character. Ramsey is definitely not a silent brooding villain. He's quite chatty.

(909) Sarah MacKeever had a very brief appearance as Selyse Baratheon early in the show. This part, once it was expanded somewhat, was played by Tara Fitzgerald.

(910) Ramin Djawadi created the iconic theme song in just a few days.

(911) A section of fans think an indication of the show's decline in writing quality in the last few seasons is illustrated by characters like Tyrion and Varys suddenly seeming less intelligent than they did in the early seasons.

(912) 49 different locations in Northern Ireland were used over the course of the show.

(913) Joffrey's Valyrian steel sword is called Widow's Wail. Of course, he never actually used it because, despite his boasts, he is a coward when it comes to battles.

(914) Peter Dinklage actually suggested his friend Lena Headey for the part of Cersei.

(915) Mark Addy said that, as flawed as was, King Robert Baratheon was actually quite a good king compared to what followed. He has a point!

(916) Kit Harington has always been keen to do a Jon Snow spin-off show which would potentially feature other characters from Game of Thrones. Sadly though, in 2024 he said the project had been put on ice indefinitely because they couldn't decide what the story should be. HBO seem more interested in Game of Thrones prequels than a Jon Snow spin-off show.

(917) A Game of Thrones still signed by Bella Ramsey can fetch over $100 online.

(918) George RR Martin heaped particular praise on Natalia Tena's performance as Osha.

(919) Season five of the show used 5,000 extras.

(920) Kit Harington said he didn't much enjoy sitting on the mechanical contraption for the dragon flying scenes.

(921) 40 different special effects were used for the digital effects over the course of Game of Thrones.

(922) Sean Bean said after leaving the show in season one he continued to keep abreast of Game of Thrones and enjoyed watching it.

(923) The Battle Of Blackwater Bay was influenced by the Second Arab Siege Of Constantinople. The Second Arab Siege of Constantinople took place in 717-718 AD, when the Umayyad Caliphate, led by Caliph Suleiman, attempted to conquer the Byzantine capital. The siege was a part of the long-standing Arab-Byzantine wars and was the second major attempt by the Arabs to take Constantinople, following the failed siege of 674-678 AD. The Arab forces, consisting of a large navy and army, besieged the city for over a year, but were ultimately unsuccessful in breaching the city's defenses. The Byzantine Emperor Leo III played a key role in defending the city, utilizing Greek Fire, a powerful incendiary weapon, to repel the Arab attacks.

(924) Tamzin Merchant, who played Daenerys in the failed pilot and was more than happy to bail when it became apparent HBO wanted to replace her, was gracious enough to later praise Emilia Clarke's performance in the role.

(925) You can see a plastic bottle by Sam's feet in The Iron Throne episode. This what they call a blooper.

(926) Oona Chaplin was originally supposed to play Jeyne Westerling but the character was changed to Talisa Maegyr.

(927) Sophie Turner said when they made season one, Sean Bean would often read the first George RR Martin book on the set between takes.

(928) Isaac Hempstead Wright started university while Game of Thrones was still on but dropped out because he didn't like all the attention. He said students would ask him for selfies as he walked to class.

(929) Game of Thrones holds the Guinness World Record for largest TV drama simulcast, with the final episode being broadcast simultaneously in 170 countries.

(930) Bella Ramsey said that when you are in Game of Thrones you want a REALLY good death scene.

(931) The production of Game of Thrones was an enormous undertaking. It involved a massive crew of over 700 people and filming in multiple countries.

(932) The showrunners said that they thought of Highgarden as sort of like being the France of the Game of Thrones world.

(933) Bronn only features in three scenes in season eight.

(934) Valar Dohaeris translates to "All men must serve."

(935) The Dothraki language was created by linguist David J. Peterson specifically for the show.

(936) Dan Weiss and David Benioff have said that, in hindsight, they should have hired more writers to help them on Game of Thrones. They said the reason they didn't is because they were inexperienced in television and didn't understand that most shows have a big writer's room to knock ideas around.

(937) For the scene where Tommen Baratheon jumps out of the window, Dean-Charles Chapman had to fall onto a crash mat which was placed above cardboard boxes. Chapman said he had to do this fall so many times his nose hurt in the end!

(938) Sean Bean said that when he watched Game of Thrones after he left the show he was of course rooting for the Starks.

(939) The character of Kevan Lannister is more prominent in the books than he was on the television show.

(940) When the last ever episode came out, Dan Weiss said he planned to avoid the internet. Given the poor reception to the episode that was a wise move!

(941) Maisie Williams met Queen Elizabeth II when the late Queen visited the set. Maisie said the Queen was very nice but it was very apparent that Her Majesty didn't watch Game of Thrones.

(942) Bella Ramsey said they got recognised in public much more for The Worst Witch than Game of Thrones. Bella thinks this was because in real life they resembled Mildred Hubble more than they did Lyanna Mormont.

(943) Ben Hawkey, who played Hot Pie, retired from acting after Game of Thrones. In 2023 he opened a London-based bakery called You Know Nothing John Dough! Direwolf loaves are a big part of the menu.

(944) You could say that season seven is a bit inconsistent in the way that Highgarden is captured easily by the Lannister army and Olenna Tyrell comments to Jamie that House Tyrell have never been good at fighting. Earlier in the show though House Tyrell is depicted to be powerful and a vital military

and economic partner.

(945) Lyanna Mormont's family sigil is a black bear in a green wood.

(946) A lot of the weapons in the show were actually made of rubber so that no one would get hurt.

(947) Sam Claflin auditioned for the part of Jon Snow. He also tested to play Viserys Targaryen.

(948) Kit Harington and Rose Leslie, who played Jon Snow and Ygritte, later got married in real life.

(949) Cersei is depicted as a more caring mother to her children in the television show than she is in the books.

(950) Dame Diana Rigg said she never watched a single episode of Game of Thrones. She did say though that she loved playing Olenna Tyrell.

(951) Natalia Tena, who played Osha, said she didn't like the way the show ended.

(952) Michael McElhatton said he didn't like the way his character Roose Bolton died. He said he would have liked a more elaborate death.

(953) Natalie Dormer is another (former) cast member who said she didn't like season eight.

(954) The Mad King, also known as King Aerys II Targaryen, was known for his descent into madness, paranoia, and cruelty, which ultimately led to his downfall and the end of his reign as king of the Seven Kingdoms. The Mad King's

actions, such as burning people alive and plotting to destroy King's Landing with wildfire, created chaos and fear throughout the realm. His erratic behavior and cruel treatment of his subjects alienated many of his allies and ultimately led to his assassination by Jaime Lannister during Robert's Rebellion.

(955) Liam Burke played the Mad King for some flashback scenes in Game of Thrones but these were never used.

(956) In the season six flashback, the Mad King was played by David Rintoul.

(957) When Sansa is on the run from Ramsay at the start of season six, Sophie Turner was instructed not to wash her hair so she'd look more bedraggled.

(958) Craster lives north of the Wall and is known for his disturbing practice of sacrificing his male children to the White Walkers. Craster also has a number of wives, who are also his daughters, and he rules over his remote homestead with an iron fist.

(959) Hannah Waddingham said she had an awful time when her character Septa Unella was 'waterboarded' by Cersei.

(960) Septa Unella and Cersei might loathe each other but Hannah Waddingham and Lena Headey are good friends in real life.

(961) Most of the actors in Game of Thrones were older than their characters in real life.

(962) There was an attempt before season six to fool people into thinking Jon Snow was really dead. What made people

dubious about this more than anything was that Kit Harington had not cut his hair nor signed up to any movie or new television show.

(963) Charles Dance said he always felt awful doing the scenes with Peter Dinklage where Tywin expresses his disappointment to Tyrion about having a dwarf for a son.

(964) Dan Weiss said that Iwan Rheon was very close to getting the part of Jon Snow.

(965) When he directed Blackwater, Neil Marshall already knew Liam Cunningham because Liam was in Neil's film Dog Soldiers.

(966) Bella Ramsey couldn't tell any friends about being cast in Game of Thrones because of an NDA with the studio HBO. A non-disclosure agreement (NDA) is a legally binding contract that establishes a confidential relationship between an employer and employee. HBO obviously have these sorts of agreements with actors to prevent any spoilers from the show leaking in advance.

(967) Sophie Turner cashed in on her Game of Thrones fame by appearing in two X-Men films as Jean Grey. It is probably safe to say though that the two films didn't get a great reception.

(968) A number of actors have appeared in both Game of thrones and Star Wars. They include Jessica Henwick, Julian Glover, Max von Sydow, Miltos Yerolemou, Thomas Brodie-Sangster, Keisha Castle-Hughes, and Emilia Clarke.

(969) The show's dragon eggs were made out of resin and covered in gold leaf.

(970) Lena Headey used a body double for Cersei's infamous "walk of shame" scene.

(971) HBO considered canceling the show after viewing the pilot episode but they decided to go ahead with it.

(972) You can buy a number of Game of Thrones themed jigsaw puzzles.

(973) We see during the Battle of Blackwater that Stannis Baratheon is a very brave leader. He is first into combat at the head of his troops.

(974) Dame Diana Rigg was one of the most celebrated 'Bond Girls' in her younger years. She played Contessa Teresa di Vicenzo, Bond's love interest (and only wife) in the 1969 James Bond film On Her Majesty's Secret Service.

(975) Bran did not appear in season five. Isaac Hempstead Wright said it was quite difficult to remember how to play Bran when he returned in season six!

(976) Mark Addy said he would have loved to have been in Game of Thrones longer as King Robert Baratheon and was sad to leave the show.

(977) Alfie Allen appeared in 47 episodes as Theon Greyjoy.

(978) Richard Madden said he watched Game of Thrones each week after he left the show in season three. Richard said when he was watching Game of Thrones he got so caught up in it he sometimes forget that he actually used to be in the show!

(979) Lyanna Mormont was only supposed to be in a couple of scenes in Game of Thrones but the producers thought that

Bella Ramsey was so good they decided to keep the character around for longer.

(980) Even though he appeared in season six as Rickon Stark, the actor Art Parkinson had no lines of dialogue after the season three episode The Rains of Castamere.

(981) Alfie Allen, who played Theon, is the brother of the singer (and actor) Lilly Allen.

(982) Millie Bobby Brown said she was 'devastated' not to get the part of Lyanna Mormont played by Bella Ramsey.

(983) Lily Allen said she turned down the part of Theon's sister in Game in Thrones but Alfie Allen said this wasn't true. She may have been joking.

(984) Game of Thrones costume designer Michele Clapton said the White Walkers were difficult to design because their costumes were a complex mix of leather and metal.

(985) The sense that season eight was rushed and too short was evident in the way that The Long Night episode wrapped up the White Walker threat. A lot of people felt that the White Walker conflict should have been an entire season - not a solitary episode.

(986) It was during the production of Battle of the Bastards that Jon Snow's return to the show (not that he was away for long as it transpired) became an open secret because Kit Harington was secretly photographed by the press shooting the battle scene.

(987) Season eight of Game of Thrones has a mediocre 55% critic score on Rotten Tomatoes. The audience score is even

worse at just 30%.

(988) An outlier in the general theory that the show went off the boil in the last few seasons is the season seven episode The Spoils of War - which has an impressive 9.7 rating on IMDB. Many consider this to be the last great episode in the show.

(989) Game of Thrones was supposed to be a co-production between HBO and the BBC but the BBC decided to pull out. That was obviously a mistake by the BBC in hindsight.

(990) Iain Glen was in 52 episodes of Game of Thrones as Ser Jorah Mormont.

(991) Liam Cunningham said the worst thing about being in Game of Thrones was the parky Northern Irish weather. He said the cast would warm themselves up with a few drinks in the bar after an outdoor shoot.

(992) In a deleted scene we see that Grand Maester Pycelle is faking his 'doddery old man' persona.

(993) Joffrey is depicted as less of a coward and more brave in the books than he was on the television show.

(994) Qyburn saving the life of the Mountain and turning him into a monster super soldier owes something to Frankenstein.

(995) Neil Fingleton, who was Britain's tallest man at 7'7, auditioned to play Gregor Clegane. He eventually took the role of Mag the Mighty, King of the Giants. Sadly, Neil passed away in 2017.

(996) Some of the plot arcs of season seven were leaked to

Reddit in 2016.

(997) Neil Marshall directed two of the most memorable episodes of Game of Thrones with Blackwater and The Watchers on the Wall. Marshall was brilliant at doing big battle scenes so it's a slight shame he didn't direct The Long Night. Marshall directed Dog Soldiers and The Descent (two excellent horror films) but his film career went off the boil in the end.

(998) Nearly 13,000 extras were used in Northern Ireland alone during the production of Game of Thrones.

(999) Game of Thrones was not an immediate hit and took a while to get some traction. It was really the death of Ned Stark which made it a big sensation everyone was talking about.

(1000) Despite its divisive final season, Game of Thrones still remains a cultural touchstone and has left a lasting impact on the world of television and popular culture. From its memorable characters to its epic battles, the show will be remembered as a groundbreaking and influential series that changed the landscape of television forever.